To John

Go on Dad...Knock!

with best wishes

Ron Clark

17/2/20

Ron Clark

Go on Dad...Knock!

Or should I? I'd come this far, and now suddenly I was racked with uncertainty.

In the rear of the car my two young daughters chanted repeatedly:

'Go on Dad...Knock!'

I was so angry with myself that after all this effort I could be so indecisive...

Ron Clark

ISBN : 978-09993116-4-6

Published by Early Girl Enterprises, LLC in the United States

Acknowledgements

Lorna Lee, Ann Clark, Dave Ward and Alison Down of the Windows Project Liverpool, Sophie Holyland.

Dedication

To those who may yet have a journey to begin,
this is mine.
To Roy, because he couldn't be there at our
journey's end.
And to Mother, Elizabeth Clark, 1918-1969

Contents

Introduction

There can't possibly be a worse way to preface a book than to make a statement like this, nevertheless here goes – I am not an author. At least I'm not a professional author.

I'm actually a garage equipment supplier. Not those 'up and over' doors outside your house, I supply equipment to the kind of garage where you take your car to be repaired. I'm the guy who sells the lifts that your car goes up and down on, the air-con equipment, the diagnostic stuff, and the (UK) MOT-testing bays for statutory annual safety tests. We supply and look after the emissions test equipment (that's our speciality) and whatever else our customers ask for. And when I say 'we,' I should confess that it's only me. When you run a tiny business, it's common practice to say 'we' so that you don't reveal how tiny your business actually is.

It's what I've done as a one-man business for close on twenty years. Before that I worked for a major company as a salesman, selling the same kind of products to the same industry as I do now, in my area, which is Merseyside, UK.

When you do my kind of work, you tend to get close to your customers. You see them often, and some become such good friends that the lines become blurred as to whether a particular person is actually a customer or a friend, because he (I deal nearly exclusively with men) has become both. When this happens, you have a good business because you spend much of your time with people who have become your friends.

It follows that you tell your customer-friends about your life, as they tell you about theirs. And you share your ups and downs, providing a shoulder to cry on (when needed), and occasionally turn to them when you need one yourself.

When I embarked on my 'journey' at the age of 42 (that culminated in the writing of this book), it followed that I shared my story with some of my 'customer-friends.' Then, following further events just a couple of years ago, two of these friends, despite not knowing each other, reacted to the experiences I described to them in exactly the same way.

My first friend, Chris Boylan, told me that I must not die without sharing my story. He said, 'Ron, you must write a book.'

'I understand why you say that Chris, but I really wouldn't know the first thing about how to write a book! I bet it would take up a huge amount of time, and I'm already busy running my business.'

'I'm serious, Ron. If for no other reason than to have a legacy to pass on to your children and family, it needs to be done.'

When my second friend, Peter Lynd, told me essentially the same thing, I began to feel a little cornered. But I also accepted that they had a point that outweighed my misgivings.

Peter couldn't begin to understand the injustice of a system where siblings are prevented from knowing of the existence of each other. He couldn't see how it could benefit anyone to be unaware of their true family. I agreed.

When you're wrapped up in a sequence of events, maybe you're not aware that it's an important story to tell because you're just trying to manage your way through it. It's your life. After listening to Chris and Peter, I could accept that my written account would form a useful and hopefully interesting legacy for my family and friends. But maybe there was an underlying message that could apply to other people, too. People who had family known to them but who, as yet, were undiscovered for whatever reason, could find something of value in my experience.

While speaking to an acquaintance about my prospective book, he informed me that he had a sister living a few miles down the road. They didn't speak. There was no particular reason why not; they had not fallen out. He told me he would love to see her, but neither would make the first move.

I asked him, 'How would you react if you only found out *today* that you had a sister you never met?'

He thought for a few moments and said, 'I would want to find her and meet her. Get to know her, I guess.'

Then I said to him, 'Yet she would be the same sister you have now that you don't speak with. Don't you want to find her, meet her and get to know her?' Somewhere in there, I believe, is my message.

So, I ask forgiveness from the outset if the manner of my writing isn't up to the standard of your favourite author. I may not possess the literary tools to replicate what they do for you. My little book could have been produced on some A4 sheets and circulated around my family and friends. Instead, I have tried to produce it as professionally as possible, within the boundaries of my capabilities, to share it with you.

All the standard caveats apply to this memoir as well as to the many written before mine. What you will read is my best effort at presenting you with the truth as I discovered and recalled it. When I was able to get permission to use real names of people or places, I did so; when I wasn't, I used my overactive imagination to conjure up creative pseudonyms to protect their anonymity. The poems you will read that foreshadow several chapters are also my work.

§§§

My journey became a lesson in how tenacity and persistence (sprinkled with a little luck) can get you to where you want to be. And how, when tenacity turned to dithering and uncertainty, 'someone' sent two little angels to get me back onto the right pathway. So, here is the story of Mother and me as truthfully as I can remember and as honestly as I can deliver. Once I began to write, my first concern was that I didn't want to write anything that would place my mother in a bad light. Throughout the turbulent years of her life, I believe that she would have wanted to do right by her family if she only could have had the support she lacked. The stigma of her single-mother status, given the morality of the time, would have only further isolated her from any possible lifelines. Her own inner demons, her inability to settle, and her run-ins with the law complicated her life and our relationship.

I have no doubt that she suffered severe depression, bi-polar disorder, or any number of mental conditions that we so easily identify and label today. I have even less doubt that she would have received no treatment for her debilitating conditions, let alone have them recognised as contributory to her situation. Mother lived in different times. Maybe the firm hand of a controlling husband would have been the solution to keep her 'in her place,' but in Mother's case, even that undesirable option wasn't available to her.

So, she lurched from one crisis to another, never settling down and rarely finding stability in her life. Anyone observing her as a mother would say she was an abject failure. Being the son who spent time with her, I was never aware of the chaos in her life. She protected me from it, and she helped shape who I am in positive ways. She didn't fail me. Because of my experiences, I'm able to pass on my precious memories of my warm, loving mother who was intelligent and articulate – the mother most people never knew.

I regret that she couldn't be around to see the outcome of my journey, because I know that only then would she realise that she did, after all, create a family to be proud of. And while it may have taken a little longer to form than the average family, this only serves to make the endgame even sweeter. Through my story, I would wish that I could give hope to those who may find themselves in a situation where they have family to find and are uncertain whether to attempt to open doors that may currently be closed. Although my story isn't a promise of a particular outcome for others, it's an honest and true story of possibilities. When I have struggled to make progress with this work, the possibility that my experiences may inspire others has been the driver that has kept me focused. So, I am truly grateful to my aforementioned customer-friends, Chris Boylan and Peter Lynd, for encouraging me to write. Both were people with whom I shared my experiences, knowing there would be a listening ear and an opinion to ponder. My dear wife Ann, whose special firebrand way of delivering constructive criticism, along with her brilliant ability to give me a woman's perspective on my story played a critical role in uncovering issues that I wouldn't have seen.

When I finally produced a rough draft of my book, I had the good fortune to turn on my radio just as an announcement was made about the 'Windows Project.' The announcer said, 'They run a "Writers Advice Desk" and are holding a session tonight, and every first Wednesday of the month, at Liverpool Central Library. All budding authors and poets may bring their work along for evaluation.' It was as though the radio presenter was speaking directly to me! Liverpool Library already held a special place in my heart as it was often a focal point during my journey. Now, it was featured again as I attempted to commit my story to print. That evening, off I went! 'Windows Project' sessions lasted no more than twenty minutes as a queue of writers waited in turn for advice. It was here that I met Alison Down and Dave Ward. Both, in their different ways, provided me with the inspiration and determination to complete my book as I attended each month.

Alison would gesture, clenching her fist and moving it from her heart to the table, 'It has to come from your heart straight onto the page. Never hold back,' she would say.

Her demonstrative nature was counterbalanced by Dave's more sober approach. 'You've done it again. The comma is outside the quotation mark!'

Dave would ultimately assist with my first edit, and I'm grateful to him for his generosity of time and talent. I learned much from Dave and Alison, and I'm fortunate to have gained their professional input.

My second stroke of luck, and third, since we could group these events together, came when I discovered Peter and Caroline O'Connor, who run Bespoke Book Covers. Not only did they ensure that my book received a cover that perfectly captured the mood of a significant moment in my story, but they introduced me to Lorna Lee. Lorna was to be the person who would prepare my manuscript for publication.

After reading her impressive credentials on her website, 'Lorna's Voice,' I asked if she would oversee my final edit. She explained to me in her colourful way how she deals with 'grammar gremlins' and 'picky punctuations' and tried politely to convince me that most authors (and therefore not just me!) need someone to prevent them from running amok in these areas. Far more than that, Lorna has, from afar, been instrumental in helping me make my little book 'the best that it can be,' and I extend my gratitude to her.

As I put my final few words into place and experience the pleasure and relief of reaching the end of my work, it's New Year's Day, 2018. Last night at midnight, from my north Liverpool home, Ann and I stepped outside to see the fireworks that were going off everywhere. It was a beautiful sight. Then, through the loud bangs of the fireworks and the sounds of celebration from nearby house parties, I picked out a distant sound that I immediately recognised. It was a sound that I had not heard since my childhood, and it filled me with emotion. It was the sound of the ships on the Mersey, blasting their New Year's greeting. Four blasts, one for each syllable: 'Hap-py-New-Year.' And in this world full of amazing shiver-down-your-spine coincidences, I realised that my writing had concluded to the very sounds that I featured where my story begins.

Go on Dad...Knock!

Night Walks

To Liverpool town in dusky fog,

All malt and hops and barking dog.

Those ships they wail such sad lament,

Four blasts – a New Year message sent.

We walk, we sing, amid the throng,

And head for home with one new song.

While through the clamour and rush the chill,

Paints frost upon the windowsill.

Then snowflakes turn to driving sleet,

Another winter's walk complete.

Bleak Mersey wind against my face,

In this, our own beloved place.

Go on Dad...Knock!

2

Chapter One: Life in the 'Tennies'

Above the fireplace, the old clock clicked and clacked towards midnight. As the hour approached, the deep haunting bass notes began to sound, one, then another, until there were too many to count. Some sounded close, some in the far distance.

It soon became a chorus, a crazed cacophony from an orchestra with no conductor. Every tune the same: two short blasts, followed by two long.

'Happy New Year'...

'Happy New Year'...

'Happy New Year'...

Outside the fog hung still. The window – partially opened to let in the sound of the celebrations from the Mersey – unwittingly allowed the bitter night air into the tiny room. Below the window, huddled under a warm blanket, Mother and I listened as the ships blasted out their noisy greeting. She turned to me and smiled.

'Happy New Year, Ronald,'

'Happy New Year, Mother,'

'Now go to sleep, and tomorrow we will go to see the ships.'

Every now and then there would be another four blasts, as if the ships were trying to outdo each other, to have the last word.

'There's another one, Mother!'

'Go to sleep now, Ronald!'

The river's sounds subsided as 1964 arrived. This year I was going to be seven!

Our tiny room offered few home comforts, the bed we lay in doubling as a settee by day. To the left of the fireplace, an old sideboard supported a large, valve–powered radio. To the right was a rickety wooden chair. The cold linoleum did nothing to warm the chill, and a light bulb hung naked from the ceiling. The dying embers of the fire had long since given up their heat, but we would be warm as we snuggled together in the bed we shared.

My mother, Elizabeth Clark, was small and slight with long dark hair. Her 46th birthday, a couple of weeks earlier, had come and gone without ceremony.

Her deep-set eyes and warm smile suggested reassurance and kindness. Calmly spoken, her soft voice was well–mannered. She called me 'Ronald,' not 'Ronnie' or 'Ron' and preferred that I call her 'Mother,' although my Liverpool accent and permanently troublesome sinuses would produce something closer to 'Mudder.'

She read to me constantly, and by the age of five or six, I was familiar with Wordsworth, Edward Lear and Walter De La Mare. I had the vivid imagination of a single child, and she did whatever she could to fuel it. She cared so much that I enjoyed reading, poetry and music.

Although we had no television, this didn't present a problem until a kid in school would ask 'Did you see *Z Cars* last night?' Once or twice I lied that I had watched a programme from the previous evening, only to be caught out because I couldn't really join in the discussion about what had happened. The smart arses knew I didn't have a telly.

Mother wanted me to appreciate the beauty of music, structure, melody and harmony. Sometimes she would combine this aspiration with her witty sense of humour. One song went something like, 'Mares eat oats and does eat oats and little lambs eat ivy' which, if sung rapidly, sounded ridiculous. Mother would always sing it as fast as she could as I giggled along. She gave the same treatment to another song about a 'Tiny house by a tiny stream in Gilly Gilly Ossenfeffer Katzenellen Bogen by the sea.' She adored Christmas carols, making me tearful when she'd sit me on her knee and sing her favourite, 'In the Bleak Midwinter.' Somehow the beauty and sadness in this carol perfectly mirrored her. For all her delightful merrymaking, there was sometimes unhappiness about her, a deeper mood behind the smiles and laughter. Occasionally she would sit, rubbing her hands together nervously, wearing an expression that suggested all wasn't right in her world. But I was far too young to understand her problems, and for me, Bleak Midwinter would become her 'theme tune,' a song that would remind me of her.

Our passion for music bonded us, and there was no shortage of it in 1960s Liverpool. The city was having its day with the rise of the Beatles, Cilla Black, and Gerry and the Pacemakers (to name a few), all based on our doorstep. The radio was always playing, providing our link to these new and exciting sounds. Our lack of a TV meant we couldn't see our heroes, and so when the movie *Hard Day's Night* appeared at the Odeon in 1964, Mother took me to see it so many times we could recite the script almost word for word. Mother had given me a musical awareness way beyond my seven years.

We were there amongst the screaming masses of fans when the Beatles came 'home' to attend a civic reception at the town hall. Mother bundled me to the front of the crowd as we hustled for a decent view from our spot outside St Luke's 'bombed out' church. As the big limos and the police outriders came into view, everyone went crazy. I glimpsed McCartney and Harrison waving like royalty as I dodged the hysterical mass of bodies screaming and collapsing in front of us. Mother enjoyed herself too, but she was older than the other girls and a bit less hysterical – it was our most exciting adventure together.

'Come on Ronald, let's go for a night walk,' she'd say most evenings. Mother could never seem to settle or relax for too long. We'd head along Suffolk Street, which had a row of Victorian houses with steep steps on one side. One had been converted into a little chip shop, *Fletchers*. They sold deep-red, crispy fish cakes, the best in town. Mother would buy one, and a big bag of chips wrapped in newspaper which she would tear open at one end to get the chips inside. She said they tasted better that way.

Then we would step out into the evening, sometimes to Pier Head with bread for the pigeons, picking our way through the evening rush down Bold Street and on beyond the railway station to Church Street passing *Woolworths* and *Coopers* with its rich aroma of coffee. It felt as if we were the only ones heading into the city as the workers and shoppers were streaming home.

She would often bring her 'Record Song Books' that contained the words to the latest hits, and we would learn a song or two by the time we got home.

We never had an umbrella, so we often got drenched. We would walk and talk as if there wasn't a care in the world, and to me, there wasn't. I was oblivious to the issues that were going on in her life.

Our walk to school each morning took us past the post office in Park Lane which was also a toy shop. The window was dressed so temptingly with an array of games and models, robots and dolls, train sets and cars. It must have been torture for Mother knowing that I would have my nose pushed up against the window each time we ventured along Park Lane, asking for another new toy. As Christmas approached the shopkeepers raised their game and made the window even more appealing. Mother would ask me what I wanted – accepting that there was no escape as I pestered her for more toys, ignorant of the pressures I was putting on her.

The toys of the time were amazing although maybe not quite politically correct. I can recall getting my own 'fireman' kit' with two big fire engines and ladders, complete with white helmet and an axe. The temptation to set the bed on fire and put my new firefighting skills to the test was overwhelming. The presentation box showed flames leaping out of a building, the ideal first toy for a budding arsonist. I also remember picking a 'jungle hunters' outfit' with lions, elephants, two pistols and a rifle to shoot them with. A belt for my pistols and a hat to keep the sun off my head meant that I was all set for a future exterminating wildlife. I also got an obligatory cowboy outfit; every kid had one, with a Stetson hat, guns and some model 'red Indians' to shoot at. If I grew up to be a danger to society, then the little post-office-turned-toy-shop on Park Lane would have a lot to answer for!

Mother did so much to make Christmas time special. We'd head to Clayton Square, a focal point in 1960s Liverpool at Christmas time. The centre of the square was roped off, and within it stood three huge Christmas trees and a large model of the nativity scene. The Salvation Army Band stood amongst the trees playing carols to shoppers who would stop by and sing along, while the 'Sally Army' man rattled the collecting tin to his captive audience. Then we'd be off to the various grottos, picking up toys and books along the way.

When Christmas Day arrived, I would rip open the mountain of presents Mother had assembled at the bottom of the bed. I went for the largest package first, usually my chosen toys from the post office. Next, I'd open my favourite Christmas annuals: Beano, Dandy and Sparky. Mother often included more 'mature' comic annuals like Eagle and Valiant, which had more stories and fewer cartoons. Then I would tackle the smaller presents, selection boxes, cloth bags full of soldiers and knights in armour, battery operated robots and Dinky cars. Mother watched intently as I ripped open my lovingly-wrapped gifts, and I knew I was a very lucky boy who believed I had everything a child of my age could possibly want.

I couldn't comprehend at the time how on earth she did it. The same kids who taunted me because we had no telly were envious when I told them what I'd got for Christmas. I wasn't old enough to understand the paradox. All I knew was that my loving Mother did everything she could to please me. My Christmases with Mother were blissfully happy times.

Home was number 62 Kent Gardens, a small dwelling within a 1930s tenement block close to China Town. We lived on the ground floor. Mother said it was preferable to living on the upper floors because the stairways stank of urine. It never bothered me. I loved running up and down the stairways and charging along the landings. Despite its slightly grim facade, the 'Tennies' in Kent Gardens had a special atmosphere. The sound of kids shouting would echo through the tunnel-like passageways. Washing would sway in the breeze on the landings while a mess of tinny radios spewed music into the air.

On Sundays, the quiet was interrupted by the bells of the Anglican Cathedral, which was only a short walk away. The road around the circular island in the middle of the tenement block allowed access to a parade of characters. The milkman was easily identified by the clanging of bottles against the clip-clopping of his carthorse early each morning. The rag-and-bone man had a distinct yell. 'Any rags?' Many a father's best suit was traded by a naughty kid for a revolving paper bird on a stick when the rag-and-bone man came round.

You could leave the front door open without a worry. People would come and go, looking out for each other through times when we didn't have a lot to lose, but what little we had was precious. These were tough, but good-hearted Liverpool people. The sounds and smells of 'Kenty' and the other tenement blocks nearby left a footprint deep in the memory of many a child brought up in the area. Including me.

We were not alone at number 62. Joseph Moore was a huge man with a problem because of the uneven length of one of his legs. To me, he was a frightening presence as he *clonk-clonked* around the place with his built-up boot that equalised his leg discrepancy. But it wasn't just his disturbing gait that unnerved me; it was his monotone, booming voice. He always seemed to be loud. Whatever unfortunate ailments Joseph Moore suffered from, whether polio or maybe a stroke, to me he was just bloody scary. His constant presence made life uncomfortable. I noticed that my poor mother couldn't settle when he was shuffling around the place. He would bark at her over trivial things that Mother did or didn't do. He treated her like his slave, summoning her by roaring '*Betty!*' followed by an instruction to do (or not do) this or that. Mother's hands would tighten into fists when she heard him bellow her name.

It was obvious that there was no love lost between them, and I avoided Joseph as much as possible, too. We spent much time walking the streets of Liverpool because the alternative was to spend our evenings in the cramped tenement in the company of Joseph. We were the mice, scurrying nervously around our little tenement that we shared with a cat.

He made her cry on at least two occasions. Once, he hit her, and she came into our little room sobbing with her hand over her eye. Another time, he attempted to kiss her. I could hear a commotion in the room next door. She came into our living room red-faced and upset.

She was embarrassed when she saw that I had heard everything, and she spat out the words, 'He's just tried to kiss me.' Bearing in mind my age at the time, heaven knows what had really happened. There was little screaming and shouting at number 62 from us, just acceptance because Joseph provided the roof over our heads, and we were his lodgers.

Being a single parent was a no-no in the 1960s, and without the support of a father figure, there was very little financial assistance to call on from elsewhere. So, when Mother was desperate for money, we would sit for hours on end waiting to be called into a little cubicle at the National Assistance Board (NAB). Sometimes she would leave empty-handed; on other occasions when she put forward a good case she might be awarded a few shillings or something towards a pair of shoes or a coat. When money was tight, there was only one place to go for clothes, shoes and the like: Paddy's Market.

Paddy's Market was a second-hand city. The iconic old place showcased the relative poverty of Liverpool life. This wasn't Marks and Spencer. It was the place to get pre-loved clothes and shoes. There were mountains of them, piled high in huge mounds around the vast expanse of the outdoor market. There was a heavenly aroma from the adjacent bakery, and Mother would treat us to a mug of hot tea before she went into battle with the sellers. Around the outskirts of the market, carpet and linoleum sellers stood on the platforms of trucks, hoping to attract attention by banging on lines of unrolled linoleum and barking out their best prices. Women in headscarves rummaged through the piles of already well-used clothing hoping to find something cheap and wearable. Much of our clothing came from there.

Whilst visiting Paddy's Market, I would meet a man called Charles Williams.

Charles Harold Williams was a tall man who wore a long coat, making him seem even taller. He appeared twice during our visits to the market; both occasions were mirror images of each other. As we made our way to the market, we passed a tenement building, and Charles emerged through the entrance gate for the encounter which was for only a minute or two. Both times he presented me with a two-shilling piece. There was no dialogue between us, no bond. It was as though the money was a grudging acceptance that I was his son, no more than that. These meetings signified the start and the end of my relationship with the man who fathered me. The next time I would meet him would be the last.

Mother made me aware that I had a sibling, Roy, but she told me that he was with family in Canada. She showed me a photo of the two of them, Roy standing head and shoulders over my diminutive mother. I didn't have the maturity to question why my brother was in Canada. I simply accepted her explanation.

I was largely unaware of other family members. Mother's contact with our family only consisted of visits to my aunts, Lily and Flo. Mother made the odd mention of others, such as Aunt Violet and Aunt Jane, but that was rare.

Mother's sister, Lily Coghlan lived in Upper Hope Place. It was situated a couple of streets along from Liverpool's Philharmonic Hall, but a world away from it. The 'Phil,' home to the Liverpool Philharmonic Orchestra and famed for its acoustic qualities, was a cultural focal point and the venue of choice for grand concerts.

A few yards away stood Aunt Lily's house. Even smaller than Mother, she had a hair lip which impeded her speech, and always wore a dark overall. Whilst I don't recall any examples of her being nasty, neither can I remember anything particularly nice about her. Her facial expression always fixed and serious, I don't think I ever saw her look happy. She was completely unlike Mother, who tended toward laughing and joking. Aunt Lily's house was dark and dreary, with very little furniture. The living room had strange, black wallpaper with white stars, making me think she might be a witch. Although Lily was Mother's favourite sister, she certainly didn't have the persona of a 'favourite aunt.' I think it's likely that Aunt Lily and Mother shared the joint spot for the role of 'Black Sheep of the Family,' and were probably looked down upon by the others.

Lily had two kids, Sandra and George. George was a livewire. He was a young scally always full of fun and mischief. But my visits to Aunt Lily were made pleasant by the presence of my elder cousin, Sandra, whom I loved. She was always so happy to see Mother and me. Sandra would take me for walks or play games around the house. She was the reason I liked going to Upper Hope Place. Mother was very fond of her, too.

We also made frequent trips to see Flo and Albert. Although I thought of them as my aunt and uncle (given our age difference), I would find out in later life that Flo was my cousin. Mother would take me to their place after school, and I would enjoy playing outside with their kids, Lorraine, Vicky and Alan.

I could only recall visiting my other aunts, Violet and Jane on one or two occasions. Violet lived in a post-war, pre-fab home in Belle Vale in South Liverpool. When I visited her and Uncle Norman, I remember being fascinated by the sight of rhubarb growing in their back garden. Norman showed it to me, and I thought it was amazing that food could grow in the ground! My inner-city life had not blessed me with much knowledge of horticulture, but my memory of that rhubarb plant was to come in useful.

My mother, Elizabeth Clark, had been one of nine siblings. She had four brothers, Peter, John, George and James, and four sisters, Mary, Jane, Lily and Violet. Peter had died at age twelve of influenza and pneumonia. Mary had passed away as a baby (only eight-months-old). They had been born to George and Mary Clark, in Liverpool, between 1906 and 1924, my mother being born in 1918, the third youngest (behind Violet and James).

Grandfather George had died in 1939, well before I was born, but I can recall my Grandmother Mary. She lived at Aunt Lily's house and cut a sad figure sat in her corner chair with a shawl around her. An earlier accident had left her with one eye, which was troubling to a kid of my age. I didn't have any kind of meaningful relationship with her. She died in 1967. I was to learn much about my various relatives later in life, but I wasn't aware of them as a boy.

In 1964, we uprooted from Kent Gardens, moving to Canning Street near to Liverpool's Anglican Cathedral. These Georgian-style grand houses, once owned by Liverpool's wealthy shipping merchants were now much more down-trodden affairs, with each house sub-divided into flats. I had no idea why we were moving, but (looking back with adult hindsight) there might have been any number of awful possibilities why we couldn't remain with Joseph Moore.

We were shown into 10 Canning Street and escorted up the grand stairs by the elderly landlady and her son. They led us into a flat on the first floor. As we entered, we stepped out of 1964 and into what seemed like 1864. The living room was gloomy, with no electricity, a couple of filthy couches and some wooden chairs.

I was shown into a separate little room with a desk, which the landlady said could be a place for me to study. Almost to demonstrate the point, she kindly lit a candle on the desk for me. But Mother wasn't happy with the lack of electricity. 'We have got our standards!' She would tell me. Then, with a whisper of a smile, 'And don't you forget it.'

We agreed to stay overnight in the dismal flat. The landlady, who seemed like a pleasant old lady, agreed to prepare something else for us. Good to her word, the next day we were moved. To the cellar.

Maybe in its day, the space was the servants' quarters. The kindest way to describe it would be an 'open plan' layout. The cramped room towards the front of the house served as a living room, a bedroom and a dining room. The window at one end of the room rose just a few inches over the pavement outside. Our view was of people's feet as they passed by the building. Stepping down to the next level was a huge Victorian kitchen. There was no WC, just an enamel bucket, but we did have the use of a large cast-iron mangle to do our wash, which was no compensation at all.

Outside, however, was the unique selling point – and I loved it. A long garden led down to a gateway at the rear of the house. This was to be our entrance and exit, and I would spend hours mucking about in the garden observing the birds and insects that visited this little haven in the city.

The cellar in Canning Street, free from the shackles of Joseph Moore, was our new home.

Only a Purse

It's only a purse from a pocket in a coat,
With a handful of coins and a ten-bob note,
A couple of keys on a plastic chain,
And an old crumpled ticket from a Lime Street train.

It's only a purse but it offers the hope,
Of a quarter of ham and a bar of soap,
For a ten-minute ride on the 82C,
To another day's wait at the NAB.

It's only a purse but it's been misplaced,
And some steps will need to be retraced,
So a hurried departure, the patter of feet,
To a flat in the basement in 10 Canning Street.

It's an urgent goodbye. It's a kiss at the door,
From a mother who just couldn't take anymore,
It's the subject of a story about to get worse,
It may never be found, but it's only a purse.

Go on Dad...Knock!

Chapter Two: The Lost Purse

There was something cosier and more comfortable about our new basement dwelling compared with Kent Gardens. The obvious difference was the lack of Joseph. We were free from his constant presence that had hung over us like a dark cloud. There would be no more fear of arriving home uncertain of the mood that would greet us. Mother and I felt happier here.

There had been no process to the move, no transportation of furniture or other belongings. We had simply left Kent Gardens, and now we were at Canning Street. The only possessions that came with us were the ones that we stood in; even my beloved toy collection had been left behind, a subject I would often whinge about to Mother. Even to a young boy, that kind of move felt odd. Maybe there were reasons why Mother couldn't go back to that place. Whatever those reasons were, she never discussed Joseph Moore again.

Our new home in the basement made no sense as a place to live. The living area was so small, and it wouldn't be too long before the situation would be compounded by a mountain of (my) toys as Mother strove to replace all the stuff left at Kent Gardens. Many years ago, this whole building would've housed a single wealthy family, now it was split into flats with different tenants on each floor. Since we were living in the cellar, there was a disparity between the sizes of our squat living area and the massive kitchen, which was originally designed to serve the entire building. The kitchen was a sight – a history lesson frozen in time. Nothing at all had been done to bring it into the twentieth century.

The huge sink had no hot water, while above it a little window framed the garden outside. Everything about the kitchen was colourless, and the grey walls lacked a lick of paint and smelled of damp. There were spiders everywhere, which I thought was great. They were the type with little round bodies and big long legs. Mother wasn't nearly as excited about the spiders as I was. The bare, stone floor meant that you needed footwear to walk in the cold kitchen. But the door from our dark kitchen led right into the garden at the back of the big house giving me easy access to hours of fun outside. Sometimes the old landlady's son would be there. I would help fill the bird feeders, and he would point out the various types of birds that visited the garden. We even had a resident robin. This was a big adventure for me after my short life in concrete 'Kenty.' I found it interesting and fun.

Nothing suggested to me that anything would change as we settled into our happy life in Canning Street. Mother made sure that I always attended school and that I enjoyed learning. I was told that I was bright by my teacher. One teacher summoned Mother to her classroom to tell Mother that she felt I was grammar school material. In reality, if I was intelligent, then it wasn't the right type of intelligence. Whatever I had, I was never going to be a top-grade academic. Passing exams wasn't my great strength.

I wasn't always the healthiest of children. I spent my fair share of time absent from school with constant ear infections and sinusitis, for which I would spend a month in hospital undergoing operations. During that time, Mother was there every day to visit me. There were no shocks or surprises, no times when Mother didn't live up to her responsibilities. We had a close and loving relationship. If we were poor, it was always masked because she was good at finding things to do to keep me happy and blissfully unaware that we were a family 'at risk.'

Mother pointed out to me that there were people worse off than us. On our way to school each morning, we were often followed by three or four kids from the same family, walking some distance behind. Mother pointed out to me, 'They don't have the luxury of being escorted by their parents, now do they? Look how young those poor children are!' I could see that the eldest boy was in my class. The others were younger still, only four or five years old.

We would stop off at the sweet shop where Mother would buy me a chocolate bar, usually a Fry's Turkish Delight. They were a lot bigger in the 1960s than they are now. One morning, I ate half of my chocolate bar and accidentally dropped the rest onto the floor. Mother told me not to pick it up, as it was dirty. Glancing behind, I saw that it was picked up and eaten by the boys. On many mornings thereafter, when she saw the same boys were behind us, Mother would buy two bars of chocolate. She would hand one to me, and place one on the floor outside the shop, telling me not to look back as they approached their gift from her. It was an example of Mother's kind-hearted nature, her way of treating the kids.

Harrington County Primary School ('Harry Board') was built in 1878. This building was part of the complex commissioned by the famous Liverpool brewer, Robert Cain. The brewery stood directly across the road from the school. Its unique old-world appearance was complemented by the heavy stench of hops and yeast giving the school an atmosphere and an aroma of its own. The smell was quite pungent yet not unpleasant, but it was always there.

Across the road from the school, there was constant shouting, banging and clanging as flat-bed trucks were loaded with barrels of ale ready for delivery to the Higson's pubs of Liverpool. From some classrooms, it was possible to watch and listen to the brewery yard activity as our lessons proceeded. When a barrel rolled down the road or fell from a crane, children in the prized classrooms-with-a-view would be treated to a bonus lesson in bawdy Anglo-Saxon English.

Harrington School had a swimming pool in the basement and both a rooftop and basement playground. When it rained, playtime would be in the basement. With its low ceiling, the racket generated by kids screaming during a rainy playtime was ear-splitting.

One day in February 1966, Mother picked me up after school and suggested that we called to see Flo. This was normal, a day at school followed by a visit to 'Auntie' Flo at Caryl Gardens. Flo was a jolly woman, and her husband Albert had a huge fish tank full of colourful tropical fish.

I was excited to arrive at Flo's place when the kids were there. We would scurry off to a patch of nearby wasteland to become soldiers or detectives hunting for clues to solve imaginary crimes. We'd have been the 'Secret Seven' had there not been only four of us, all on a scruffy patch of wasteland on Caryl Street, near to the Royal Southern Hospital.

We arrived at Flo's place as usual. The kids and I legged off as normal. But on my return to the flat, I was surprised to find that Mother wasn't there.

Flo informed me that Mother had misplaced her purse. She had left to retrace her steps and return home in the hope that she had left it there. 'She'll come back for you later, Ronnie, when she finds it.' Flo smiled and offered us a snack. But I wasn't hungry. Apart from school, Mother had never left me anywhere before. I was concerned (and a bit annoyed) that she had gone without me.

Many hours passed. Mother didn't return. Flo and Albert decided that I must stay put until she came back. We must have looked out of their window every two minutes, but there was no sign of Mother. The kids encouraged me to play, but I could only think about my missing Mother. From the other room, there was much-hushed adult discussion as Flo and Albert became increasingly concerned.

'If she doesn't return soon we'll have to contact the police. It shouldn't take this long to find her purse.' Flo paced from the settee to the window. Back and forth. 'It's getting dark outside'.

'Whether she finds it or not, she left Ronnie here. She should've come back by now. What'll we do if she has buggered off and left him?' Albert drummed his fingers on the kitchen table. 'She could've taken him with her to find her purse. Something's not right.' He looked at me, and then turned away, shaking his head.

Flo was doing her best to keep me re-assured, but I could hear them discussing their suspicions. Flo came back into the living room.

'I'm sure your mum will come back soon Ronnie,' she said, unconvincingly, her pinched features and constant looking toward the window giving away her real feelings.

Albert stood behind Flo with his arms folded, looking serious.

'I want my mum. I want to go home.' I repeated, not accepting Flo's attempts to comfort me.

I had never known what it was to be without Mother, least of all have her disappear on me. At eight-years-old, I was unable to comprehend the issues that may have been weighing down on

32

Mother. From my little-boy perspective, our life together was so simple, so straightforward, so happy.

But in retrospect, Mother's life was anything but simple. Even the things that were known to me at the time could have stories behind them. Why had we left Kent Gardens? Why so quickly? Did she not have the means to pay the rent? Where was Charles Williams in all this? What was the real story of Roy, my sibling, allegedly in Canada, why would he not be here with Mother? Was her financial situation so bad that she couldn't stay at Kent Gardens, and now maybe the same was happening at Canning Street? All of these were valid questions, but none of them would cross my young mind at the time.

Mother didn't come back that night. I spent the night wailing 'I want my Mother,' crying into a tear-soaked pillow. However sympathetic they may have been, I must have driven Flo and her family crazy.

Morning came. I knew that for Mother to be missing overnight something very bad must have happened. Flo told me I was to stay with them and not go to school.

I spent my time in limbo hoping desperately for the knock on the door that would signal Mother's return. It never came. The family tried to maintain some degree of normality for me. A week passed without any further developments, and I was becoming increasingly distraught and lost.

§§§

One day I was glued to the window, sobbing and hoping that Mother would appear when I saw a shiny black car pull up on the street near the front of the tenement block. Two smartly-dressed men stepped out. Moments later they were knocking on the door. They were coming for me.

There was hushed conversation coming from Flo's kitchen. Again, I had the uneasy feeling that the conversation was about me. The kitchen door opened, and the men came into the living room. One of the men was slim with a smart suit. He towered over the other, shorter man who had a happy, smiling face.

'Hello, Ronald,' beamed the smaller man. He looked kind and smiled as he spoke, attempting to lighten the mood, I suppose. 'My friend and I going to take you to your new home.'

I wanted to be sick. 'I don't want to go to a new home. I want my mum'.

I was a sensitive child and understood what they were doing. They wanted to make this 'new home' sound like a wonderful proposition, but it wasn't going to work on me. They might as well have smiled and told me they were going to take me to the dentist to have my teeth pulled.

'I don't want to go. I want to stay here until Mother comes back so she knows where to find me'.

Flo stood over me, crying. I knew this situation wasn't of her making. Albert stood alongside her, arms crossed in front of his chest like he was in charge, but silent.

Then the other man, the tall man with the smart suit, spoke up. 'You can come with us in our new car. You can see it through the window, look!'

Nothing mattered. I was hearing, but I wasn't listening. Nothing felt real anymore.

'Come on Son, we have to go.' Both men rose from the settee, and the smaller man took my hand. Albert opened the door as Flo sat and sobbed.

35

Flo had done her best, but she already had many mouths to feed. She had no choice but to inform the authorities to arrange for me to be taken into care since it appeared increasingly unlikely that Mother was going to return.

I was being taken away from my family altogether. This was to be my first journey in a car, but rather than excitement, I was filled with fear and apprehension as the men led me out of the 'Tennies' at Caryl Gardens into their shiny black car. They let me sit in the front, and the tall man who was driving showed me how to take the handbrake off before we drove away, up Hill Street. He explained to me about the gears as we speeded up. I was momentarily distracted from my situation by the kindness of the men who had come to take me away from Flo's place and everything I knew.

But what were they taking me to? I had no idea.

Girl's Shoes

It's very hard to find new friends
If you cannot conform
The way you speak the way you dress
It has to be the norm

You're gonna to get a rotten time
You're gonna get the blues
And you're gonna get in trouble
If you wear girl's shoes

You'll get it in the playground
You'll get it in the street
You'll get in assembly
The library and the loos
The teacher will be mad at 'cha
The girls will chuck a bag at 'cha
The kids ain't gonna like you
If you wear girl's shoes

You gotta be mistaken if you think you're wearing those
Your parents need to understand you need boy's clothes
You're gonna get a rotten time
You're gonna get the blues
The teacher's gonna cane yer
If you wear girl's shoes

You'll get it in the playground
You'll get it in the street
You'll get in assembly
The library and the loos
The teacher will be mad at 'cha
The girls will chuck a bag at 'cha
The kids ain't gonna like you
If you wear girl's shoes

Go on Dad...Knock!

Chapter Three: A New Life

It was Thursday, February 17, 1966, and I had no idea where I was being taken to. In fact, my first-ever car trip took about thirty minutes, ending in Speke, a housing estate to the south of Liverpool. We pulled in outside a row of tidy-looking houses. I was escorted up the path to what was to be my new home. We were met at the door by a chubby woman with sharp features. Her smile wasn't warm and friendly like Mother's.

'Come in Ronald,' she beckoned. We entered the hallway. As she spoke to my 'chaperones,' I noticed that she had a strange accent. 'Hellor...narce dare intit?'

Her voice was loud and piercing, and I couldn't understand what she was saying. She was more 'domineering matron' than 'cuddly mum.'

I didn't like her. If Annie Foy was to be my new parent, she wasn't anything like Mother.

Once inside the living room, she introduced me to her son, Stephen. He looked to be about my age and seeing him took away some of my earlier apprehensions when I entered Annie's house. Stephen was friendly, and before too long we were watching television and chatting.

The Foy household was luxurious compared to what I had known before. They had a living room, a kitchen, and a front room which they referred to as the 'parlour!'

Upstairs, there were three bedrooms, a bathroom and a toilet, much different from the enamel bucket that Mother and I had endured in Canning Street. They didn't appear to have a mangle, though.

There was a long garden at the rear of the house, with a swing. A swing! And they even had an outside toilet. I couldn't grasp how these people had two toilets when Mother and I only had one enamel bucket. That was unfair.

The Foys had a television, too. I thought about the kids back in Harry Board and all the TV programmes they talked about in school like *Mr Ed* and *My Favourite Martian*. Maybe they would let me watch these TV shows so I could talk intelligently about them with my mates. That bit of joy lasted only a moment, though. I wasn't going to be able to tell my friends in Harry Board. I wondered, *would I ever get to see them again?* At least the realisation that I would be able to watch TV brought some positivity to my childish mind that was otherwise filled with trepidation.

Later that evening Joey Foy, Annie's husband, arrived home. He was a dock worker at Liverpool's 'South End' dock yards. He looked tired and dirty. Joey was a small, chunky man – tough but likeable.

I had been aware of his untidy appearance when he arrived home, but he was also aware of mine. 'Your hair is a disgrace,' he commented. 'We'll soon sort that out'. He winked at me.

That evening he cut my hair, and he laughed as he described my hair as being 'like rat's tails.' I hadn't arrived in Speke in good shape.

I immediately liked Joey, although, I'm not sure that he was the driving force behind Annie's wish to keep foster children. Joey would've been busy enough working hard on the docks, but his 'anything for a quiet life' nature meant that he probably allowed Annie to have her way. He was a simple man who had served in the navy, his uniformed picture proudly displayed on the wall. He liked a pint and could entertain by singing and playing his piano accordion at the local British Legion Club, where he was popular.

For my first few days at the Foy's, I was inconsolable at the loss of Mother, spending most of my time crying and asking if she was going to be coming back for me. There was still no word, no update on her situation. Annie would send me out to play with Stephen. The newness of my situation would temporarily take my mind off Mother. Then I would think of Mother and be upset all over again as a pang of despair washed over me. My grief was still raw.

Despite my negative first impressions, Annie Foy did what she could to be kind and help me settle in, but I didn't want to be there. I wanted to go home. Their lifestyle was so different from anything I had been used to. Mother and I were quiet and reserved, while the Foys didn't seem to be happy unless they were arguing with each other. Annie was strict, supervising everything I did. Clothes had to be neatly folded over a chair before bed, and she was already giving me chores, like washing dishes and running to the shops for her. At first, I enjoyed the challenge, but in the coming weeks, my willing nature turned me into a bit of an errand boy.

My previous lack of physical interaction with other kids meant I didn't play football or other outdoor games well. I was very overweight, too. Mrs Foy would encourage me to go out to play with Stephen and his friends, but I wasn't built for the physical life that these kids led.

When I did go out to play football, I would huff and puff around, hopeless at running and tackling. I hated having the piss taken out of me because I couldn't do the things that came so easily to these budding athletes.

In my 'past life,' I would have spent leisure time reading or listening to the radio. There was no chance of that in this noisy household. Annie bawled her disapproval of one thing or another in a seemingly permanent state of annoyance infused with anger. And doing things on my agenda was no longer an option. Mother always would ask me what *I* wanted to do, whereas here, I did as I was told.

Against this background, however, there was much to like about my new environment.

We lived on the road that linked Speke to the picturesque little village of Hale, with its thatched cottages, blacksmith's barn and a police station that was basically a house with a policeman living in it. The Childe of Hale pub celebrated the life of John Middleton, a sixteenth-century giant who was allegedly nine-feet-three-inches tall. His cottage was a few feet along the lane from the pub. Farther down in the quaint churchyard was Middleton's much-visited grave. The lane continued onto Hale Lighthouse, overlooking the Mersey estuary.

Across the road from my new home was a large area of woodland. Behind the woods, the Airport runway ran parallel to the river. Farther up along the road, the 'Dam Woods' sat behind well-manicured playing fields, an area of preserved ancient woodland with tall trees and small brooks alive with frogs and newts. Speke in 1966 was a lovely place; I simply hadn't settled into it because of the circumstances that brought me here.

After a few days settling into my new environment, it was time for school.

Stocktonwood County Primary was completely unlike my big, old-fashioned 'Harry Board.' It was far more modern and had a huge playing field surrounding it. My first day, however, was anything but a bag of laughs. It was memorable but for all the wrong reasons.

I had arrived at Speke in the clothes I stood in. No one noticed that I had been given the wrong shoes when I was collected from Flo's place. Unfortunately, I was wearing girl's shoes. Soon after arriving at the schoolyard I had attracted a crowd of kids who formed a circle around me pointing and laughing.

They chanted 'Girl's Shoes' in uncanny unison. I stood surrounded by this mob of kids until eventually a playground attendant saw the commotion and broke up my unwanted induction ceremony.

Never having experienced this kind of situation before, I allowed the crowd to poke fun at me. I just stood there with my head down, waiting for them to stop. The kids in 'Harry Board' were from a tough area, but they were my mates. I should have done more to stand up for myself, but it wasn't in my nature.

It was a not a good start, and for days and weeks afterwards, I was referred to as 'Girl's Shoes' rather than my name. This was a new era, and I was learning fast. I was the foster kid. Any shoes would do.

Within a few days of arriving at Speke, I was visited by my social worker, a likeable lady called Miss Hughes. She offered to take me to the city on a shopping trip. Miss Hughes also had a car. I was beginning to get used to this new way of getting around!

She told me, 'I would like to take you to town. We will get you some nice new clothes, and then we will have some lunch.' Maybe she had been alerted to my footwear *faux pas* a few days earlier.

Miss Hughes was pleasant and easy to talk to. A thirty-something, she was smart and good looking with dark curly hair. On the drive to town, she chatted with me about my situation. 'How are you settling in Ronnie? Mr and Mrs Foy are nice people'.

I didn't respond. Not even a shrug. It's not that I didn't like the Foys. They *were* nice people. But I didn't want to accept that this was my new life. I wanted to be back to my normal life with Mother. Nobody would even talk to me about Mother. Everyone seemed to be distancing me from the possibility of life back with her. Why didn't anyone understand how much I missed her?

Later, in the café of the department store, Miss Hughes ordered tea and chocolate cake.

'I want to go home Miss Hughes.' I said, my tongue loosened by her kind gestures.

'That may not be possible just yet Ronnie, so you really do need to get used to your new home.' Her eyes and voice were so kind that it was difficult to reconcile her denial of my request with her compassion. Usually, when anyone told me 'no,' the message was delivered abruptly and with no room for misinterpretation.

Miss Hughes continued, 'Mr and Mrs Foy will look after you well, and it will be just like having a new brother, too. These people are called "foster parents" Ronnie,' she explained. 'They will take care of you until we find your mum. Right now, we cannot say how long this will take.'

She reached over and gently placed her hand on one of arms. 'Ronnie, be nice and try to fit in. Not all foster homes are the same as yours, and not all children are treated as well as you will be. You really must do your best to accept your situation.' She smiled and nodded as if doing so would make me agree.

It worked. I nodded, reluctantly, bought by Miss Hughes's kindness, logic and lashings of chocolate cake.

'Now don't forget what I have told you,' she re-iterated, as she returned me to Hale Road.

'Okay, Miss Hughes. I won't.'

The message hit home. She was letting me know that things could be worse. I was smart enough to understand that the way forward was to embrace my situation and accept it for what it was.

Over time I began to fit in at Stockonwood School. I had a good sense of humour, and my ability to be self-deprecating was making me popular. At playtime when the kids lined up to be picked for a game of football, I would be picked first, and we'd all laugh. Everyone knew that I was hopeless at sports.

I would go on to make some terrific mates, including Doug Hesketh who would become a friend for life.

§§§

One of my class teachers, Jim Lyons, picked up on my ability to write poetry and encouraged me to do well at it. Mr Lyons asked me to write a book of poems. He gave me some outline ideas and suggested I produce work relevant to the subjects he suggested, like 'Appreciation,' and a poem describing the scene at Jesus' crucifixion.

When I produced the work, the school entered it into a national literary competition: 'A Book of Verse by Ronald Clark aged 10, A Pupil at Stocktonwood County Primary.' I won a national Brooke Bond prize for the school. Having my writing recognized and appreciated was a turning point for me.

When the big news broke that I had won a prize, I was called to the stage at a school assembly to receive my award. I received a big round of applause from the teachers and pupils. Rather than being ridiculed as I was in the past, I was respected for my literary skills. My new-found status as 'Poet

Laureate' for Stocktonwood School would elevate my status to prefect which meant taking on 'important' responsibilities. Mine was to guard the loos at playtime to deter smokers and graffiti artists. I was beginning to go places.

A new social worker began visiting me every three months or so. He was Mr Wilson. Middle-aged and very well spoken, he had a moustache and thick-rimmed glasses. Although he was always polite, he had an air of authority about him like a headmaster.

He was different than my previous visitor, always wanting to talk to me privately about my personal happiness and my progress at school. He wanted to drill deeper into my situation than Miss Hughes did. And Annie didn't like it one bit.

He and Annie didn't see eye to eye. Whenever she knew he was coming, she would make disparaging remarks about him. 'That Mr Wilson. I'd be careful what you say round him. You see how he has his little book and writes everything down, Ronnie? What does an old man like him know about raising children, anyway?'

I didn't know what to say, so I would shrug or nod or shake my head – whatever was appropriate to show Annie that I was on her side. I can't say that I was, but I knew my life would be so much easier if she thought I was.

Annie was reluctant to let me out of her sight when Mr Wilson was around. She would hover, repeatedly asking him, 'Would you like a cuppa?'

'Thank you, but no, Mrs Foy. This is my time to talk with Ronald *alone*.' He was courteous but firm. By then I had developed a sense of something between loyalty and obedience to Annie, without being fond of her. But her cleverly chosen words prior to Mr Wilson's visit would ensure that I would 'say the right things' when asked. She made sure to tell me that other foster kids under her wing had been 'sent back – and we didn't want that, did we, Ronnie?'

A pretty, young girl called Julie had been brought into care with Annie some months after I arrived. But she was unceremoniously returned to the authorities for getting up in the middle of the night to 'steal' a fairy cake from the larder. That set the benchmark for behaviour that wouldn't be tolerated, and I made sure I didn't nick a fairy cake, mindful of the horrors if I was sent elsewhere, as described by Miss Hughes. I didn't realise it at the time, but Mr Wilson was an extremely intuitive man, more than capable of reading between the lines. He was picking up on factors that were having a negative effect on my life and my progress.

I overheard him discuss my progress with Annie one day. He had arrived unannounced, thereby guaranteeing that Annie would be annoyed with him.

'I've come to talk about Ronald's work at school'.

'How do you mean, his work at school?' Annie replied, on the defensive from the off, when there was nothing to defend.

I could tell that he was trying to prompt agreement from her that my progress in English and poetry were noteworthy and to see that she would encourage my development in these areas.

It wasn't to be.

'I see Ronald is doing well and has gained an award for his poetry work. Maybe this is something we need to take note of and look to develop?'

Mr Wilson was very softly spoken. It was easy to confuse his politeness with weakness, which is what Annie did. The resultant scene was embarrassing as he gently tried to lead her to the correct response, which he didn't get.

'Poetry, what do you mean? Who the bloody hell wants to read poetry?' She shook her head, reacting as if Mr Wilson had told her I had a knack for making balloon animals that I could turn into a lucrative career.

'It's a special gift, and it needs to be nurtured. You should encourage him to join the local library where there may be writers' groups to help develop his skills.'

'Yes, and what will *that* cost?' Annie responded, arms tightly crossed in front of her. 'And who will pay?'

The objective of the meeting was lost as soon as Annie got angry.

Annie continued her tirade. 'I still can't get money for that new mattress that I had to pay out for, and all you want to do is come here to talk about *poetry*?' Her voice had risen. She made 'poetry' sound like a dirty word.

Annie reduced the conversation to something she understood: the practicalities of day-to-day living and the money that makes living possible.

Mr Wilson sighed. Loudly. He probably realized that he wasn't going to achieve anything but irritate Annie further. He stood and fixed his hat to his head. His face was strained. 'Well, I suppose that will be all for today then, Mrs Foy.'

She nodded almost imperceptibly. Mr Wilson left, leaving me sat on the settee, my head spinning with bewilderment at the confrontation that had taken place simply because I was showing some early aptitude for poetry.

The gloomy mood hanging over the living room was punctuated by the sound of Annie, still angry, as she banged and clashed dishes around in the kitchen.

I was in a complicated triangle of mind games in which Mr Wilson was trying to do the best for me, Annie was trying to do the best for herself, and out of misplaced loyalty and fear of the alternatives, I was forever saying the 'right' things to be supportive of Annie. Had I pushed the button, I would have been moved to a different home. But I was always mindful of Miss Hughes' warning.

Then one day, Annie gave me the most amazing news. Mother had been in touch!

She wanted to see me. Annie made it clear that she wasn't coming to take me back, but she was coming to visit me. I was over the moon.

Annie made me look nice and presentable. My heart was racing as the time got nearer. I stood guard at the window to make sure I wouldn't somehow miss her. Suddenly, I saw her! Her walk was distinctive, so recognising her from way down the road was easy. Yes, that was Mother: small and fragile in her headscarf and long dark coat. The doorbell rang, and there she was. Her dark clothing contrasted against her warm smile. It was such a happy moment! But something wasn't quite right. The day was gloomy, overcast. There was an unexplainable strangeness seeing Mother in the Foy's house. Somehow these two different aspects of my life didn't belong together.

Annie fussed about making tea and Mother sat on the living room couch with me alongside her. I could see her looking around, observing the material things that were now part of my environment: the relative normality of the home with a television, gardens, the swings, and my new companion, Stephen.

But once we had hugged and cried and sat together there was an uneasy feeling in the room that was created by the presence of Annie. I soon realised that there was a competition going on, and I was the prize. I had expected to be talking to Mother alone. I wanted to know how she was and where she was living. Was she still in Canning Street? What had she been doing all this time that she had been away? Was she going to take me home?

Instead, Annie began telling Mother how well I was doing here – at school, with my new brother Stephen, with my new friends and how much we were all looking forward to the holidays booked to Wales.

'Ronald is doing well. He is very happy here. Very happy, aren't you Ronald?'

'Yes, Auntie Annie.'

Mother sat silently, listening.

'He's even won a prize in school. What's it for again, Ronald?'

'Poetry, Auntie Annie.'

'Well done, Ronald!' Mother beamed.

Before I had a chance to revel in the glow of Mother's pride, Annie cut in. 'And we'll soon be going on holiday! We've just bought him his holiday clothes.' Annie disappeared upstairs momentarily, fetching the T-shirts and trousers to display to Mother.

While she was upstairs, Mother and I stared at each other, smiling uneasily. It was as though we were in the same room but miles apart, unable to have the conversation I wanted to have, as Annie dominated the proceedings. Before either of us could break the spell Annie had cast, she returned.

Mother turned her attention to Annie. 'Thank you for everything you're doing for Ronald. I know he's happy here with you. I couldn't possibly provide for him in the way that you do.' Mother looked right into Annie's eyes when she said this. I could tell she meant every word.

Then Mother looked at me. Her upturned mouth shaped a smile, but I could see the sadness in her eyes. 'Ronnie, I see how much you've grown and how well you look under Mrs Foy's care.' She turned away from me and continued. 'You'll grow up with everything you need here and make all of us proud.'

This was the moment that my future was sealed. If there had been any intention of talks to reconcile me with Mother, they were not to be. If Mother had come to visit me with a view to taking me back, Annie had presented her with a dilemma. If Mother cared about me, she would now realise that Annie could provide a better life for me than she could. She would have to sacrifice her personal wishes for the good of her son; otherwise, she would be adding to the evidence of her ineptitude as a parent. But Mother was a splendid parent. She wasn't thinking about herself; she was thinking only about me. And maybe, just maybe, Annie was right. It wasn't possible to know if Mother could have coped with the responsibility of taking me back.

Annie had sold the idea to Mother that this was the ideal place for me to be, and Mother bought it.

§§§

My weight had dropped off as I persisted playing football and legging it around the wood with Stephen and our gang of mates, so I was a picture of good health.

When Mother visited again some weeks later, we took a walk to Central Parade, the main shopping centre in Speke. It was lovely to walk and talk again with her. Yet as we wandered around the various shops, buying sweets and cakes to take back, I became sad. This wasn't anything like our time together before she left me. We were together again, but it was no longer just us. I had to go back to my new home which didn't include my mum. As we walked back, Mother re-iterated Annie's words from our first meeting. 'Ronald, I'm so pleased that you appear to be in a very good home, with nice people.' She grabbed my hand a gave it a squeeze.

I smiled, nodded, and squeezed her hand in response. That's not what I wanted to do. Inside, I was shouting, 'Mother, I belong with you, not her. I promise I won't be any trouble to you. Please take me with you. Please don't leave me again!' But my little-boy mind was still afraid of disobeying Annie, and something about Mother had changed. I was afraid of being too much of a burden to her in whatever new life she was living. All these thoughts stopped me from telling her how I really felt.

It followed that the thing that was missing from our conversations was my honesty. Mother wanted to hear that I was happy where I was. So I told her what I believed she wanted to hear.

She took me back to the Foy's and stayed for a short while drinking tea and chatting. When she stood to put on her long black coat and headscarf and said goodbye, I tried not to show how I felt. I watched her walk down the pathway with her lovely, familiar little stooped walk. She turned to wave goodbye. I wanted to scream, 'Wait! Let me come with you.' Instead, I waved back.

Mother continued to visit on two or three occasions. Although I loved to see her, the pattern of my feelings would always be the same. I was strangely sad to see her arrive because I knew we would play out the false act that I was doing fine without her, never saying how I really felt. Then I would have to suffer the emptiness of seeing her leave again – I always held out hope, though. *Maybe next time she visits, it'll be to say that her life is sorted out and we're going to get back together again...*

But one day, everything changed.

On 12 March 1969, I returned from school having spent the afternoon in woodwork class making a device called a matchbox holder. My creation held a box of matches, and it worked by pushing the box down over the holder which exposed ready-to-use matches. Unless a person lost the ability to open a simple matchbox, my project was totally useless. Nonetheless, I was proud of my piece of work and arrived home to present it to my foster parents, both smokers.

I walked into the living room where I came across a scene that I wasn't expecting. Mr Wilson was sat on the couch holding a cup of tea. He had a serious look on his face. Annie Foy was standing in front of the fireplace, puffing on a cigarette. As I entered the room, she turned and switched off the television.

'Sit down, Ronald.'

'Look, I made this in school for you and Uncle Joey.' I thrust the matchbox holder into Annie's hand. I sensed that there was something wrong. Annie didn't pay any attention to my gift.

'Mr Wilson has come to see you, Ronald. Sit down, please. He needs to talk to you'.

'Look, Mr Wilson. I've made a matchbox holder.'

Mr Wilson smiled briefly, politely taking hold of the matchbox holder and surveying it before placing it on the arm of the settee. He cleared his throat. 'I'm afraid I have some very bad news for you,' said Mr Wilson. He clasped his hands together.

Silence.

Why do people tell you they have bad news and make you wait before they tell you? In the moments of heavy stillness that passed, my imagination ran wild, but I didn't conjure the scenario he finally presented.

'I'm sorry, but I have to tell you that your mother has died.'

I sat there, unable to move. My mind seemed to stop working, too.

Annie moved over to me and placed her hand on my shoulder.

'She died yesterday, in hospital,' he explained. 'She had been very unwell, and...unfortunately, she has passed away.' Mr Wilson stared intently at me.

There was another awkward silence.

Annie was staring, too. They awaited my reaction.

They didn't get one. Outside, the sudden sound of laughter shattered the silence as kids pushed a steering cart past the house.

Annie offered to make more tea.

It was the toughest moment of my short life as it became clear to me that I was never going to see Mother again. I tried not to cry in front of the two adults, overly sensitive to how this would be perceived by Annie Foy. I believed she would interpret my grief as an act of disloyalty. I was wrong. Annie wasn't such a bad person. I was simply confused by the occasions when Annie had seemed to compete with Mother over me. My experiences seemed to have given me inner mental strength, and I could cry when it suited me, bottling my emotions rather than being upset spontaneously (as should have been the case).

In the reports that I would read many years later, Mr Wilson had noted my seeming indifference to Mother's death. To him, it was so noticeable that he had warned Annie Foy to be aware that there may be a delayed reaction. This wasn't the case because it wasn't delayed in the first place. There had simply been no witnesses. Mr Wilson would later note that there had been no delayed reaction, and this was interpreted as my no longer caring about Mother. He couldn't have been more wrong. My mother's death broke my heart. I expressed my anguish privately: in my room or during walks around the empty playing fields at Dunlop's factory.

On the morning of Mother's funeral, I was sent to school as usual, along with a note for my teacher, asking if I could be excused school for the day so that I might attend the funeral. I had also been given bus fare. This would get me to Upper Hope Place, Aunt Lily's home, from where the funeral would proceed. Off I went to school, note in hand. At 9:30 am precisely, I was excused and allowed to leave to take a bus to say my final goodbye to Mother.

But it wasn't to be.

Arriving at Auntie Lily's, I was surprised to see my father, Charles Williams, amongst the small gathering of people, some of whom I didn't know. This was to be the third and last time I would ever see him. I made my way into the spartanly-furnished back room with its witchy wallpaper hoping to see Sandra, but she wasn't there. Charles Williams popped his head into the room and told me it would be better if I didn't attend the funeral after all. I had to obey. Once again, grieving the loss of Mother was a private affair. I sat and waited for the group to return. When they did, I took a bus back to Speke.

In the years ahead, I would wonder about Mother's passing, I was never properly informed about what had happened to her. In my early teens, I had been upstairs in my room, getting ready to go out with friends, when I overheard a conversation taking place in the living room below. My foster parents were discussing Mother's death with visitors. They said that there was a rumour that her death was 'suspicious.' They were speaking quietly, knowing that I was in the house. I wanted to find out more about this rumour, but I doubted that anyone in the house would tell me. I kept thinking, *this is nothing like what Mr Wilson told me about how she died. He wouldn't lie to me, would he?*

So, the rumour would stay locked in my memory for years to come.

Go on Dad...Knock!

Chapter 4: No Drama

By the time I got to secondary school, I had pretty much completed my transition from an overweight and immobile boy into a fully-formed Speke kid, skinny and agile. I was better able to hold my own even if that simply meant I could run fast when being chased. The shy, unassuming Ronald was fading away, too, and I became more than capable of handing out a bit of cheek to score points in the company of my schoolmates.

The cultural pastimes that Mother had tried hard to instil in me were becoming obsolete through lack of use. No longer reading, writing or listening to music, I spent my spare time charging around the woods, playing footy on the fields and sometimes dodging gangs of lads visiting the area to see who was 'hardest.'

The deep scar on the back of my head from an assault with a house brick served to prove that at least one gang was much harder and faster than we were. The woodland opposite our house was a brilliant place for kids, but it was territorial. When strangers came along, violence was never far away. I learned quickly that you didn't get anywhere by writing interlopers a poem.

Altercations would start with a hurried bang on the front door, followed by the war cry, 'There're some lads in the woods!' It was the equivalent of an air raid siren; a call to arms to grab your weapons and chase away the intruders. There we stood lined up on the roadside, our gang. As we hurled stones into the bushes that formed the woodland directly in front of us, we listened for the yell as a stone hit its target. Often there was no one to warn off. False alarms raised by bored kids with nothing better to do were just part of the gang life.

My life in Speke had represented a significant change in my lifestyle. By no means was it all bad. I was never going to be a real 'hard knock' like many of my contemporaries, but at least I was a bit tougher, more streetwise and fitter than when I had arrived.

My foster brother, Stephen, was a year my senior, but a foot shorter than I was. He was a fearless little bugger. In his efforts to toughen me up, he led by example. When he took me to the baths to teach me to swim, his method was simple. He repeatedly pushed me into the water until, eventually, I could swim. I was bloody scared not to!

One day, following a visit to Speke baths, we called to the cafe upstairs for hot chocolate as we often did before leaving. A large spiral staircase ran from outside the cafe to the ground floor. At the top of the stairs were a couple of local 'hard knocks.' One of them gave me a shove as I walked out of the cafe door. They must have thought I was alone. Then Stephen walked out behind me. Suddenly the 'hard knock' found himself lying at the bottom of the spiral staircase. His mate ran away before he suffered the same fate. Stephen took no messing, and the message was clear: don't mess with Ronnie, or you might have Stephen to answer to. Meanwhile, I was about to get an opportunity to return to slightly less aggressive activities.

One morning I was walking into school when I received a sharp tap on the back of the head. Not a house brick this time, thankfully. The perpetrator of the 'assault' was Tony Eustance, our teacher for P.E. and drama.

'I expect to see you at drama group after hours, next Thursday!'

I was intrigued and excited. *Why me?* Everyone knew that the drama group at Speke Comprehensive was something special. Although I was apprehensive, I knew instinctively that I wanted to be part of it.

The drama group was known to be a select bunch. I had never been chosen to be part of anything like that before, so I rushed home to tell Annie Foy my good news and to ask if I could be late home from school for one evening each week.

I was twelve-years-old, and the school was only a five-minute walk away, but my proposal wasn't well received. Annie wasn't at all impressed. 'Drama... what do you want to do that for?' She looked as if she had just taken a big whiff of spoilt milk. I don't think she expected an answer to her question.

My initial enthusiasm quickly turned to embarrassment. I stood red-faced wishing I hadn't asked. She didn't make clear whether she was going to allow me to go, instead choosing to make disparaging remarks about my request. I felt uneasy and confused.

It wasn't unusual for there to be an uncomfortable atmosphere at home. Annie lived life under a constant cloud of annoyance. I tried my best not to add to her frustrations, but this time, I did.

Her unexpected response to my request made me feel silly as I wrestled to see her point of view. There was no one around to be on my side about the drama group, to tell me that I wasn't doing anything wrong. When Thursday evening came, I was unsure where I stood with her, but I was so keen to attend that I stayed back at school taking my chance that there would be no repercussions when I got home late.

I fitted in immediately with the drama group. This was something I felt I could be good at, and I had loved my first evening class.

We performed an improvisation of Jackson in the Waxworks. Mr Eustance gave me the part of Jackson, locked inside the waxworks at midnight as the scary 'models' came to life. It was a brilliant experience, and I loved every minute of it. Drama – performance – was for me.

But I ran into a different kind of drama upon arriving home later. Annie Foy was livid. She was an ominous storm cloud hovering around the house, waiting to burst. Annie treated my attendance as an act of defiance, of betrayal. I didn't know how I'd be able to continue if I was going to have to weather that kind of storm every week. Despite her continued resistance, I attended each Thursday evening, offsetting the enjoyment against the reaction I got on returning home.

Over time I had shown some promise in the group, but it was necessary to stay committed because we were rehearsing for the next productions. Mr Eustance had to decide who among would be assigned parts to play. When this happened, there would be more classes, more late evenings. I was fearful of getting too deeply involved then having to quit because of Annie. Sad to say, Joey wasn't much help either. He couldn't see any reason to support my new-found passion. Instead, he took Annie's side. 'Ronnie, you don't want to be hanging round with that lot. They're nothing but a bunch of pansies. How's bloody drama going to help anyone get a proper job?'

I continued to defy their opposition, ultimately taking part in a couple of the school's major productions – 'Massacre at Peterloo' and 'Cyrano de Bergerac' – finding my place in the 'midstream' of the group which consisted of some supremely talented actors. It was a brilliant experience to be acting alongside them.

'The Crucible' was our next production. Mr Eustance was talking to the group with a view to distributing the various parts to the players. I told Annie that I might be given a part in another play; it would mean more rehearsals and more late evenings. This time she hit the roof. 'I'm fed up with this bloody drama,' she roared, and let me know in no uncertain terms that the time had come to pack it in.

Some days later, Mr Eustance was taking our P.E. class. We were using the running track near the woodland where I lived. As we jogged around the track, Mr Eustance ran alongside me and mentioned that he was allocating parts for 'The Crucible' and had something in mind for me. I should have been excited, but I was heartbroken.

I told him I no longer wanted to be involved in the group. My eyes teared up. I tried to keep running, but I was too choked to speak. When he asked me for a reason, I didn't respond. After an awkward moment, Mr Eustance ran on ahead. I'm sure he was bewildered by *my* apparent choice to suddenly cut my ties to his drama group without any explanation.

That was the end of my dramatic 'career.' Annie had decided that it had to end, and it was futile to continue resisting her. She got her way, but I disliked her for what she had done. Meanwhile and unbeknown to me at the time, my social worker, Mr Wilson, had been keeping a keen eye on my progress in the drama group. He had even visited the school to see how far my dramatic 'career' might progress. It was years later that I would learn just how much effort this man had put in behind the scenes to try to support me.

Mr Wilson didn't know that Annie had directly put a stop to my involvement with drama. In keeping with my inability to turn on her, I didn't tell him. And, like Mr Eustance, he must have been left bewildered by 'my' choice. Nothing could alter the fact that for a few short years in the early 1970s, Speke Comprehensive School stood out as a beacon for drama, and a force for good that assisted the positive development of many young people. No less than fourteen pupils would go on to become members of the National Youth Theatre. Many years later, a number of us would collectively put our stories together, forward them to Her Majesty's representatives and make a proposal that succeeded in recognising the achievements of our amazing mentor: Anthony Eustance, MBE.

Mr Wilson had known of my wish to stay on to sixth form at school, noting that he was glad that I wanted to do this. Once again, this ambition fell at the first hurdle. Instead, Annie decided that I was to leave school at the end of year four. 'Better that he goes to work straightaway and earns his keep.' And so, at fourteen-years-ten-months-old, I was summoned by Mr Lawson, our Careers Officer whose job it was to pretend to care about our future prospects. He suggested that I attend the careers office in nearby Garston which I did that same day.

There, I was asked if I fancied a job as a trainee chef at Liverpool Airport. Imagine that, a chef!

I had no idea whether this would be the career for me, but off I went to the airport. At the end of the interview, I was offered the job. Simple, all done in a day. *Maybe Annie will be happy with this news.*

'Start a week Monday,' said my interviewer, Mr Smith.

On Monday, I proudly marched into the airport reception area and up the stairs to the place where I had interviewed so successfully a few days earlier.

'Who are you?' asked the first senior person to see me.

'I'm Ron Clark, and I've come to start work as a trainee chef for Mr Smith.'

'Don't think so. He's left the Company,' replied the man as he shook his head. 'And we don't know anything about you.'

So, my career as a chef ended before it began. *Ah well,* I thought, *I don't want to be a chef anyway.* Years later, the irony of my 'nearly career' in catering would be the subject of some fun with someone I had yet to meet.

After a short time working as a labourer for a building contractor, I started work as an apprentice motor mechanic at a car dealership in Liverpool. Around the same time my school friend, Doug Hesketh, had come up with one of his 'ideas.' 'Why don't we start a band?' Doug asked with his trademark mischievous look.

There were lots of reasons why we couldn't and shouldn't start a band. We had absolutely no money, no equipment and nowhere to rehearse. Oh, and neither of us had any musical talent. None. We had both recently started work, and so we had little free time to acquire basic music abilities or organise a band. But Doug was never one to let reality stand in the way of a good dream. We started a band.

We recruited some schoolmates to our fantasy island project and began to assemble an array of musical instruments. We bought some cheap 'copy' guitars from Frank Hessey's music store in Liverpool. (Don't scoff; this is where the Beatles began!) Before long we were blasting out songs by Status Quo and Rod Stewart from our 'studio' – Doug's mum's attic.

Gerneth Road in Speke had either the most tolerant neighbours on the planet, or the most inebriated ones. Otherwise, they surely couldn't have endured the horrible din that our early practices generated. Amazingly, it wasn't too long before we were gigging 'live.' Our first live appearance at the Metal Box club was quite a success.

It gave us the taste for band life, and we continued to play and improve together right into our early twenties. Doug was to meet his future wife, Angie, who, along with her sister, Gloria, would come to watch us play at the Moonstone Pub in Liverpool, an iconic haunt for the hippie types and progressive rock fans in the city during the early 1970s.

Meanwhile, Annie's resistance to things she didn't approve of had softened. I was now working, and we had established a much better relationship. Annie and Joey would pick on my long hair and hippy lifestyle, but it wasn't malicious; they were just poking fun.

Joey loved to call us all drug-crazed hippies. Annie enthusiastically agreed. Some of his favourite rants were nothing short of hilarious. 'Who the hell is that "Wizard?" You're not telling me he's *not* on drugs!' (Google Roy Wood if you are below 40).

Joey would change the words of songs and band names. My favourite band, Wishbone Ash, became Wishbone Harry, taking everything to the level of an act in a Liverpool Dockers Club. It was funny, and we would all share the joke.

My time with Annie and Joey spanned 20 years with all the highs and lows of any family. With the passage of time, I grew fond of them. I know they grew fond of me, too.

It's true that Annie was often a thorn in the side of my development, but it's also true that she was responsible for providing me with a home and stability that many in my position would have envied. I grew fond of her, as I always had been of Joey, accepting her for who she was with gratitude for the positive things that she had brought to my life. For my part, I didn't leave them at the first opportunity. Instead, I made it my business to stay with them and support them as they were growing older.

Stephen and I grew up together as real brothers. We were so close that no one ever questioned why we had different surnames when referring to each other as 'Our Kid.' We had been (and would continue to be) around for each other.

Joey Foy died at home from lung cancer in 1985. Annie would pass away the following year after a stroke. Shortly before Annie's death, I married my first wife, Sandra, in May 1986, at the age of 28. The wedding was a thoroughly lop-sided occasion, with Sandra's large family on one side and my relative (my brother, Steve) on the other.

In 1987 my first daughter, Laura, was born, followed by Amanda in 1988. As I reflected on my own early years, I promised my babies that their upbringing would be happy and untroubled. I was proud that I had, at last, established a family of my own.

My 'band-mate,' Doug, and Angie had married, and along with her sister, Gloria, and Gloria's husband, Ian, they migrated to Perth, Australia along with some other old school friends. My wife wouldn't give up her family ties, and so we didn't take up Doug's invitation to join them. I was sad to see them go and promised that one day I would get to Australia to see them all again.

We moved to a leafy suburb of south Liverpool, as by now I was an area sales engineer for a company selling automotive diagnostic equipment, the type of thing once referred to as 'Crypton tuners' (ask your dad!). I loved the job and worked for the company for eleven years. I had made a life and a family with my wife and kids. My in-laws, Sylvia and Ted, had become people I also loved, respected and looked up to as parents.

Go on Dad...Knock!

'Window'

And as you walked to school that day

A message in your DNA

Sent from Mother

And through my girl

A window, opened into my world.

Go on Dad...Knock!

Chapter Five: A Grim Discovery

'Alping, Alpong or Alpung? I need an answer.'

'Alping, Daddy,' groaned Laura, her young face sternly set in response to the stupidity of the question. She'd heard it all before.

'What about you, Mand?'

'Alpong please, Daddy.'

'Ah, good choice!'

I rattled the contents of the box of Alpen into their bowls, the same cereal for both. It was 1999. The girls were growing up so fast. Laura at twelve was already developing the dreaded pre-teenage attitude; Amanda, eleven, was still sweet and caring. This morning would be my turn to walk them the short distance to school.

As the girls spotted their friends and rushed off to meet them, I would stand, wave and feel a deep pang of sadness as I watched them leave my world and enter their world of school. I knew that I would be forgotten the instant they saw their schoolmates – a moment's parental jealousy.

On this particular day as I stood waving, I hesitated a little longer to watch as they strolled into the school building. I noticed for the first time that Amanda walked with a distinct style, a very slight, barely-noticeable lean. As I watched her, I felt a sense of *déjà vu*. I had watched someone walk away from me with exactly that style.

I returned home, still pondering over the mysterious person that my daughter was unwittingly reminding me of. I stared at a newspaper, unable to read it, as my mind wandered. Then it came to me in a flash. A shiver ran down my spine. Mother!

It should've been immediately obvious, but it wasn't. It had been 31 years since she had passed away. I was now 42. As I reflected on this sudden connection with my memory, it felt as though I was receiving a message, a reminder from the past that Mother was my daughter's grandmother.

Maybe it was a wake-up call to pass on to my children the story of Mother – my life with and without her – but I had little evidence of her. I didn't even have a photograph. I should know more about my mother's life and death, if not for me then for my girls. Years had passed, and I had not taken the time to find the answers to what had happened to her. There was no excuse for that.

I would sometimes reflect on my early life with her, notably at Christmas time, when I would take the girls to Liverpool Cathedral, hoping to instil in them the same love for the atmosphere of Christmas that she had given to me. The beautiful sound of the choir would always remind me of her. If they sang 'Bleak Midwinter,' I would struggle to contain my emotions. On the girls' birthdays, I would be thinking how proud she would have been of them. There were also times that I thought about my lack of blood family – how unfair it was that my daughters only had 'one side.' Although Sandra's lovely family helped compensate for the imbalance, the facts remained.

How on earth I had got to this age without doing anything to find out more about Mother was suddenly weighing heavily. I decided to research Mother's death, but I had little idea where or how to begin.

I wasn't sure that I could get a death certificate because I didn't know the exact date of her death. I found myself at the Liverpool Central Library where I had heard there was a family history department. Maybe they could give me some advice. When I called there, a couple of elderly gentlemen explained to me what the facilities of the library had to offer. I was particularly intrigued to find that it was possible to view pages from old local newspapers that had been stored on microfiche films. Annie Foy's whispered comments about Mother's suspicious death never left my mind. If something awful had happened to Mother, then I reasoned there was a strong possibility that it would have made the newspapers, specifically, the *Liverpool Echo*.

I had a lot of ground to cover, and so three or four times a week I attended the library after work. I would have been eleven years old when Mother died in 1969, but I couldn't remember the month. So, I viewed the pages of every daily newspaper from my birthday month of August 1968 to August 1969.

I searched every page of every edition, checking from front to back, scrutinising the 'births, deaths and marriage' sections and the first few pages of news. Then on to the next day, and so on. I found nothing. In one sense this came as something of a relief, but I still had no answers to my questions.

I accepted that I would have to obtain a copy of her death certificate. So, I headed to Brougham Terrace, the registry office for births, deaths and marriages.

When I arrived, there were several long queues of people. They seemed mainly to be asking for replacement birth certificates for passports, and their requests were being dealt with very quickly. It bothered me that my enquiry might need a bit of work. I worried that I might be dismissed as the staff worked their way efficiently through the long line of people dealing with relatively simple requests.

My turn came. I almost apologetically addressed the young lady. 'I'm trying to find the cause of my mother's death, so I need her death certificate, but I only have a general date when this might have been, and little more detail other than my mother's name.' I could hear myself rambling.

The woman nodded, asked for the sketchy information I had and jotted it down. She disappeared into the rear of the building, returning some time later with the news that there was no sign of a death certificate for Mother. I was pleased that I had found someone helpful, but she had not got a result. She came out and chatted with me, telling me her name was Pamela. 'It's strange that we don't have your mum's death certificate, even given your inability to give me her exact date of death. Would you give me some time and call back again in a few days? I need to do some digging.'

'Oh, yes! Thank you so much. You've been more than kind.'

I went back a few days later. She told me there was no progress.

I was desperate to hang on to this helpful girl who was trying to assist me, sensing that if I lost her interest, it might be difficult to make any further headway. When she asked me for further details of Mother's death, I told her as much as I knew of the story, which was very little. I let her know that I had overheard conversations that implied there might have been more to her death than I had been allowed to know.

She came up with a suggestion. 'I have friends at the Coroner's Office. I'll get in touch with them, and let you know if they have any details about your mum's death.' A few days later, I received a phone call from Pamela. There was news. Her contact at the Coroner's Office had been in touch with her to say that they had found information about Mother.

They wanted me to call them to arrange an appointment. I did. 'Bring someone along for support,' the person suggested. While that sounded ominous, I decided to go alone. A few days later, I made my way to the Coroner's Office. I was greeted by two male clerks and guided into a room where they offered me coffee and advised me that I was going to be given information that I would find distressing.

I nodded. 'Please, just share with me what you discovered.'

They produced a file. As they placed it on the table in front of me, one of them informed me that my mother had taken her own life. Of all the possibilities I had conjured when I was younger about how she had died, suicide had never crossed my mind. I had no idea that she was capable of such a thing. I felt sick.

They poured coffee as they gave me time to digest the initial shock of the information. Then they continued to inform me of the details. Mother's body had been discovered in the basement of 248 Catharine Street, Liverpool. She was found on a chair in a recessed area like a pantry, where she had taken an overdose of barbiturates. A newspaper under the chair was five weeks older than the date she had been found, and the coroners had confirmed that she had been there, unnoticed, for about that length of time.

How could she lay dead for so long without being missed?

The clerks were gentle and empathetic, offering me time to stay and read the documentation. They said I could make copies that I could take away with me. I was made aware that there were photographs of my deceased mother at the scene, and that I could have them if I wished. I declined the offer. The realisation of her lonely and pitiful end left me numb. I realised why I had been advised to bring someone along for support.

I had in front of me a copy of the autopsy, the police report and the findings from the inquest, and to my horror, Mother's suicide note. I noticed that the writing started in pen and some way through switched to pencil.

The letter was an attack on my father, Charles Williams. 'I have nothing to live for now,' it began, going on to say that he had promised to marry her but had instead thrown her out when she ran out of money. 'I have two children to him, one twenty-nine and one eleven years old,' she wrote.

Now I was shocked for a different reason. Two children! Did she mean Roy? 'This man has a habit of living off what he can squeeze from a woman,' she went on. 'When the money goes – out goes the woman, it happened to me before, eleven years ago and now I am almost certain that I am pregnant again but he couldn't care less'...The 'eleven-year' reference appeared to suggest that he had thrown her out of the home when I was born.

I tried to visualise her fumbling around for a pencil when her pen had failed her at the moment she was about to take her life. How thoroughly depressed and abandoned she must have felt to put herself through this.

Who was this 29-year-old 'child?' What little she told me of Roy didn't put him eighteen years my senior. The overload of information made it hard to focus on any one part of this increasingly mystifying puzzle. I began to read the inquest notes. They were dated 12 March 1969. The statement was from my father, Charles Williams. He stated that he was a retired hotel storeman who lived at 248 Catharine Street. 'The deceased, Elizabeth Clark, wasn't related to me but I had known her for about thirty years. She was aged 50, a domestic worker, and had no fixed abode. We had lived together, off and on, for the past thirty years. The first period was for twelve months when she left me for some years, and after that, she would return to me for short periods and go away again for long periods. There are two children of the union. A girl aged thirty years and a boy of about ten years, who is now adopted. We had been together since November of last year, and I last saw her alive about five weeks ago, when I left her in the house.

94

'When I returned about four hours later I found a note on the mantelpiece which said 'Dear Charles, I'm sorry I have to leave you like this. Tell my sister Lily, I have been a burden to her and would she forgive me?'

'On 11th March, when workmen were clearing out the flat below, I was called down and told that a woman's body had been found in the cellar. The police were informed, and when they arrived I went down with them and saw the deceased sitting in a chair in a corner of the cellar; there was a plastic bag covering part of her head. I later identified the body to Sergeant French.

'Her general health had been good and her sight as normal, but her hearing was deteriorating. During the last two weeks, she had complained of headaches, which were severe, and had diarrhoea, and had seen Doctor McIntyre of Chatham Street who had prescribed sleeping tablets for her.

'During our last period together, she had been very depressed and had talked about committing suicide by throwing herself under a car or a bus.'

As I read the notes, a confusion of issues raced through my mind. Even during these raw moments as I digested the information put before me, I sensed that some things didn't sit quite right. How could the note that Mother left for Charles Williams be so warm, addressing him as 'Dear Charles' when later that day she would take her life and call him 'fit to burn' in her suicide note?

There was no sentiment shown towards Mother from Charles Williams in the inquest notes, no regret that this had happened, just a feeling that he was distancing himself from the relationship. Mother's suicide note was there for all to see, but was the 'Dear Charles' note seen at the inquest? Surely there were grounds to question the difference in sentiment between the two notes.

Mother's suicide note referred to Charles William's address, stating 'His name is Charles Williams, and he lives at 248 Catharine Street.' Yet Mother was at 248 Catharine Street when she died. The house was number 248, and it was sub-let into various dwellings. Charles Williams lived in an upstairs flat, and Mother died in a basement flat, all within number 248. Why, therefore, would she state his full address on her suicide note if she was actually at the premises at the time that she wrote it?

She need only have written that he lives 'upstairs.' This cast doubt in my mind that she wrote the note whilst in the basement. Could it be that she wrote it earlier, or somewhere other than at number 248?

My poor mother had been found with a plastic bag pulled tightly over her head to the bridge of her nose. It's difficult enough for me to imagine her putting herself through this miserable process, but I'm at a loss to imagine how she could do this to herself after taking a large overdose of tablets. I wondered if I was asking the same questions that my foster parents had been asking all those years ago. I could see how there were questions that had remained unanswered at the inquest, although surely now it was far too late to ask them. I had not had any contact with Charles Williams since the day I saw him at Mother's funeral, many years ago. I didn't know his whereabouts, or whether he was alive or dead.

The place where Mother suffered her tragic death was no more than a few paces away from our earlier home in Canning Street, where Mother and I shared our happiest times. I wondered if we had moved there so that she could be near to him, although, at the time, I had no knowledge that he was in her life.

Now, all these years on, I had further questions.

Why, if I had a sister, as these notes seemed to suggest, had I not been informed? Surely Social Services wouldn't keep this information from me? I took a bus home, and before it arrived at my stop, I decided I was going to find my sister.

Chapter Six: Go on Dad...Knock!

Energised by the idea of finding my sibling, a myriad of emotions swirled around constantly in my mind. Negative thoughts: fear of the unknown, of opening doors that once opened, can't be closed. Positive thoughts: optimism and anticipation; who is she and where is she?

I was angry, too, and my anger turned to the authorities that had been responsible for me in early life. I tried to understand why this information would be kept from me. It crossed my mind that the people who 'play God' in Social Services must themselves finish work in the evening and head off to be with their own families. Whether perfect or imperfect, a family is what it is, and must surely be too precious a commodity to tinker with – to airbrush out one member or another, to censure relationships.

Any sentence that begins, 'We didn't tell you about the existence of your sister' can't be finished with a valid reason. How can it? I felt that I'd been relegated to a lower level of humanity, handed a different set of rules than those applied to 'normal' people, by those in authority willing to forget the values that apply so preciously to their own lives.

Whilst Social Services were never to blame for the circumstances that fragmented my family, no value had been placed on helping us to at least be aware of each other, so that one day it could be possible to establish our relationship, our family (such as it is).

To be made aware that you have a sibling at a time of life when you are reconciled with the idea of having none is a hammer blow. It presents difficult questions. Are things better left alone given the passage of time? My instincts said no. I wanted to find her.

Impossible as it was, I tried to build a picture of her in my mind. According to the notes from the inquest, she was eighteen years my senior. I imagined what it might have been like having her in my life through my timeline. When I was ten, she would've been twenty-eight, and so on. I tried to visualise what it could've meant to have an older sister in my life.

During my school years, I was always envious when I'd visit friends, seeing the link between brothers and sisters, the similarities both visually and through their behaviour. How lovely it must be to be 'like' someone else. Then the bigger questions would haunt me: what was her relationship with our mother like, how well did she know her, and what were the circumstances that led her to be elsewhere, never in my life?

I had gained experience in doing the type of detective work needed, and I understood the formula a little. But I had no name, no address, no clues (except her age) about her. The Coroner's report had been specific about that, she was eighteen years my senior. This meant she had been born in 1939, give or take a year.

I recalled a statement made by my foster parent, Annie, in my early teenage years, 'Ronnie, you have an older sister somewhere. Her name is Georgina or something like that.' I had not taken the comment seriously. She mentioned Georgina in a throw-away fashion – as a piece of trivia – rather than the important revelation it should've been. Now, it was important news. I can't speak for other eighteen-year-olds, but at that age, I wasn't particularly astute or tenacious. Since Annie didn't offer any more information, I didn't pursue the matter. It didn't register with me that Annie could've been telling me something of immense importance.

I accept a certain amount of guilt for not being more pro-active when hearing about Georgina, but was it my job to find a sister I never knew about simply on the casual word of a foster parent? Wasn't that Mr Wilson's job or his agency's job? If a foster child like me had family, wasn't their job to reunite me with them? It seemed if as they were pretty good at *placing* children in care but not so good at *getting them out* of the system back to their real families.

As an adult, Annie Foy's revelation took on meaning; it was a thread of evidence, my second clue. I could put the name and age together and make a start, but where to start? For some time, I flailed around trying to connect with someone who could help. I wrote to the police, believing that they would have records of Mother's suicide. Perhaps the authorities contacted my sister about the death. If they had, I might discover an address or something useful.

Their response was to tell me that they had no records of her death. Even if they did, they wouldn't be able to provide me with any information about anyone involved in the events. Why? Data protection. 'We cannot tell you about any event that involved anyone other than yourself.' Who makes this stuff up? I wrote to the Salvation Army. They needed details I couldn't provide to proceed. I also wrote to Social Services. They sent me a single A4 sheet of information. It confirmed what I had learned at the Coroner's Office, but with a further twist. One of the sentences read, 'According to Mrs Parr, the Mother's sister who was interviewed after the death, there were four other children, a girl born in 1939, a boy two years later, and twins, half Chinese, whose ages were not given.

'There are no details about these children on file.'

Suddenly I was reading that I had even more siblings. More shock and another mystery. This time there was no clue as to the age of the twins. The fact they were half Chinese suggested further potential problems. Who was their father? What were their names? Were they living in China? As I processed the information, I decided that I should continue with the search for my eldest sister to see where it led. Maybe then I would get more information about my ever-increasing family.

I knew about Liverpool City Library's family history department all too well. It was there that I had started the search for the information about Mother, and so it seemed logical that I needed to revisit the library, this time with my new mission. The obvious difficulty when trying to trace a woman is that, beyond a certain age, she is likely to have married and changed her surname. If this were the case, there would be no point in searching directly for the Clark name. But this also presented an opportunity, albeit one that would require many hours of slogging through historical records.

I decided that I would use the marriage records at the library and calculate the likely years that she may have married (age eighteen to twenty-five). I could've been wrong, but it was necessary to start somewhere.

So, I made a calculation based on her birthday in 1939. She may have married between two dates, 1957 and 1964. I also assumed the name Georgina was correct, having nothing else to go on.

Off I went to the library, where I searched the micro-fiche for all the marriages of G. Clark between the years 1957 and 1964. Any I found, I took to Brougham Terrace to see if I could reference the birth date of the bride with my sister's birth year. My search for Georgina didn't produce any results, so I decided that rather than give up, I would try variations of the name.

I recalled that my foster parent was vague when she mentioned the name of my alleged sister all those years ago. It had been a case of: 'I think you might have a sister, and I think her name might be Georgina.' The obvious variations to the name were Jean, Jane or Gina. I decided to try again using J. Clark over the same span of years.

However random it may sound, I tried a name that was different to the name suggested so fleetingly by Annie all those years ago. Over a few visits to the library, I produced details of four marriages that were possible suspects.

The entries listed on the micro-fiche had no forenames, just initials, then surnames and the date, but tellingly they would state if the wedding was in South Liverpool, the most likely area for my potential sister to have been wed.

Having sourced four possibilities of women with the name of Jean Clark marrying between 1958 and 1965, the next step was to attempt to match the age of the bride and to see if there were any parental clues on the marriage certificates.

The next stop was my old friends at Brougham Terrace, the Registry Office for Births, Deaths and Marriages. There, I reacquainted myself with my old contact Pamela, explaining what I was trying to achieve this time. I hoped I hadn't exhausted my 'credit' with Pamela, who had already gone beyond the call of duty when she helped me find the information regarding Mother's death. Thankfully, she remained interested in my journey and was happy to help me again.

I left her with the details, and she promised to contact me with any results she might find. Three months had passed since my first visit to Liverpool Library, ending with the short list of possibilities that could lead to my sister.

It was equally possible that I could be completely wrong, following leads that led down blind alleys. Yet just like the time I started my quest for information about my Mother's death, I seemed to take a little step of progress forward with each visit, one clue always leading to another.

Weeks passed with no word from Brougham Terrace. I was becoming pessimistic and uncertain what to do if this line of enquiry failed. I feared that, after the holiday, Pamela may have got fed up with me and failed to pursue my request. I had taken a long shot with my unfound sister's forename and made assumptions about when, and where, she may have married, if indeed she had married at all. Any one of those assumptions could be completely wrong, so my pessimism was justified.

Yet there I was, Christmas Eve morning, and the phone rang. It was Pamela! 'Ron, I think we have a match.' One of the marriages was of a Jean Clark to

Alan Reay, in 1964, and the entry on the certificate showed Jean as being 24, the probable year of birth being 1939. The father's name had been left off the marriage certificate. Pamela had then obtained the birth certificate for Jean, finding the mother to be Elizabeth, and father's name not entered, just as on mine.

Surely this was her! It was a miracle that we had got here with so little to go on. I thanked Pamela once again for her support, her matter-of-fact approach belying the reality that she was taking part in events that were potentially life-changing to me.

Suddenly I was excited; I had a feeling of momentum. And the fact that it was Christmas Eve made it seem somehow more appropriate that I should give this one big push.

I now had names, date of birth and marriage dates, but where was she? I thought about her name – Jean Clark – and already felt an affinity for her because it just sounded right. But I needed to be careful not to build up my hopes.

There was one slight possibility that I could find an address for these people. I needed another miracle. If you don't believe in long shots, look away now! Some weeks earlier I explained to a friend about my quest to find my sister, and he loaned me a CD containing names and addresses for the entire population of the UK believing it might help me at some point. The software he loaned to me was a demo version. This 'try before you buy' CD didn't contain information about everyone in the UK, but it still had a massive database of names and addresses of the UK population.

It would've been of little use had we been searching for someone called Clark. But Reay? There wouldn't be quite so many of them. I loaded the CD and narrowed the search to 'Reay, Merseyside.' Within a split second there it was in front of me: J & A Reay, Coral Avenue, Huyton.

A shiver ran down my spine.

I was certain that I was now looking at my sister's address. Ironically, it was only a ten or fifteen minutes' drive away from my home. My heart told me that this was it, but my head told me that it might not be.

§§§

The software didn't display a forename, just an initial. Even if the forenames were correct, it still could be someone other than my sister. I had been down many wrong roads before. I needed to be sure. Only the electoral register would clarify the full names. I needed to check at the library, but it was Christmas Eve.

My daughters Laura and Amanda had heard my conversation with Pamela, and subsequently with my wife, Sandra. The excitement of the moment was affecting them, too. Now they wanted to come with me, excited by the idea of finding my sister, their aunt on 'Dad's side.' Taking the girls was likely to slow me down, but I agreed that they could come. The city centre was crazy with shoppers rushing about for last-minute gifts. Parking was a nightmare. Time was moving on, and I knew the Library might well close early. I wanted to check the electoral role for Coral Avenue, to verify the forenames before I attempted to contact them. Bundling the kids up the staircase with me, I requested the electoral register for Coral Avenue, Huyton.

'Very sorry, Huyton is in Knowsley Borough, this is Liverpool. You need Huyton Library.'

DAMN! I should've known that. Rushing back to the car, I headed to Huyton Library, a drive of about twenty minutes from the city centre.

When I arrived, I was informed that they no longer had copies of the electoral register for the area; it was elsewhere. Because of this, I couldn't get the final clarification I needed that the forenames at the address were Jean and Alan.

I realised that I was being picky by trying to be definitive. I also accepted that the right answer was simply to call their house and ask if it was them. After all, I was now in Huyton, minutes from the address, and the surnames and initials added up. I questioned whether I was just putting obstacles in my own way, putting off the decision to just go to the house.

Once again, I bundled my poor children into the car. We were off on another mission, this time to bite the bullet and go directly to Coral Avenue. As I pulled onto the road, I felt my heart speed up and my mouth go dry. I crawled along the road until I could see that we were getting close to the house number I had hastily scrawled down on a post-it note.

Two or three doors before it, a man and woman were outside in their front garden brushing the path. I pulled in and wound down my window.

'Excuse me, I'm looking for Jean and Alan's house. Is that it with the blue door?'

'Yes, that's it,' the man replied.

My question had been answered. I had clarified their forenames. I knew it was them only three doors away. I had almost certainly found my sister's house. Christ.

I pulled in. The car door felt like lead as I finally pushed it open. I left the car, paused for a moment and got back in it again. I was racked with uncertainty. Sensing my indecision, my two young daughters began to chant:

'Go on Dad! Knock!'

'Go on Dad...KNOCK!'

They couldn't understand the possible implications of what I was about to do, and I was annoyed with myself for being so indecisive. Taking a deep breath, I smiled at my girls, screwed up all my courage, and pushed that lead-filled car door open one more time. I made my way up the short path to the door; the sound of the girls chanting in the car rung in my ears, spurring me on.

I was acutely aware that I was at one of life's crossroads. What I was about to do would have an impact on my family and other people, people that I had yet to meet.

I took another deep breath, rapped on the door, and took a step back. A man opened the door. Alan. His calm demeanour was reassuring as I greeted him. I had prepared a couple of questions that felt right to ask. Being on the doorstep, I felt awkward and intrusive asking such personal questions.

'Hi, may I ask is your name Alan, and is your wife Jean?'

'Yes.'

'And was she born on 24th April 1939?'

'Yes, she was.'

'Then I believe I'm her brother. Would you mind if I said hello?'

He paused for an uncomfortable moment before he said with a soft, welcoming voice, 'You had better come in then.'

The outer facade of the house had been that of a simple terraced Merseyside dwelling, but inside the small living room, there was a homey feel, like a quaint country cottage brimming with trinkets. The window ledge was covered in decorative paperweights, and there were shiny brass ornaments around the fireplace. A gallery of pictures and photographs adorned the walls, and there, sat on the couch, was Jean.

I started to explain, 'Hi Jean, I'm your brother, I understand you probably weren't even aware of me, but look, I have your birth certificate here, and mine. Here's our mum's. I've got stuff here about our father...' I was all over the place, babbling and failing to deliver my explanations in a way that anyone could possibly understand.

Jean sat before me, staring at me, obviously shocked but smiling. We all did our fair share of gazing at each other for a few moments. Her demeanour took away all my previous concerns about the type of person she might be. Her pleasant expression and ready smile made me feel silly that I had been so apprehensive about meeting her, and I could instantly see the similarities in our appearance.

She listened carefully to what I had to say, and as I calmed down and started to explain myself in a more composed manner, she became tearful and emotional.

She revealed that she had no idea that I existed. I guess I wasn't the only one kept in the dark about my siblings. Jean informed me that she, too, had lived in Speke. Her address was just a short walk from my own in Hale Road. This revelation alone meant we had much in common, so much to discuss. I showed her the evidence of our relationship: my birth certificate and other documents that proved our connection. I showed her the details from Mother's inquest and the statement that our parents had siblings. As we talked, I realised that I had completely forgotten that the kids were still outside in the car!

I ran out and brought them inside, introducing her to her new little nieces Laura and Amanda. She brought out a large tin of Quality Street. As she began to share the sweets with them, I felt a wave of pride and happiness. I was 42. Jean was 60. We were meeting for the first time, and our connection was immediate. It felt like we had known each other all our lives as we shared these special moments.

Next morning, Christmas morning, after a night reflecting on the events of the previous day, I staggered downstairs to the sound of wrapping paper being unceremoniously ripped from boxes, followed by the 'whoop whooping' of joy as the contents were revealed. I wasn't in great shape following too many glasses of Liebfraumilch the previous night, but the hangover was put on hold for a while.

Laura and Amanda had risen before me, and I was annoyed with myself since I loved to see the look on the girls' faces on Christmas morning as they attacked their presents.

At 8:30 am, the telephone rang.

'Good morning, Brother Ronnie. I've had a good cry now – Merry Christmas to you all.'

Chapter Seven: Just Off to See a Friend

It was indeed a Merry Christmas. Much of it was spent reflecting on the overwhelming events of the previous day. 'You've got a new sister for Christmas, Daddy,' chanted my girls, charmingly. I constantly replayed the scene from Jean's house in my mind: my misplaced apprehension and how all my concerns had melted the moment I set eyes on Alan and Jean. It had been a day that would stay with me forever.

Whilst in Jean's house I had spotted a picture on the wall of her son, Alan. It had delighted me. I had looked so like my newly-acquired nephew when I was a similar age. In years gone by, I had been so envious of school friends who had family with whom they shared characteristics. Not everyone has siblings, but to have neither siblings nor parents is a little isolating. Yet in the space of one day this sense of being singular vanished. I saw for the first time that I, too, had a sister and family who resembled me. If only I had known.

And why hadn't I known? Why was Jean a secret that I had to work so hard to uncover? Yes, I had 'missed a trick' when, years ago, Annie Foy had suggested to me that I had a sister. Maybe, therefore, the fault was mine. Or perhaps when you are fostered, the authorities suggest to your foster parents that they might pass some fleeting remark about a sibling (or other real family member) that you are not aware of. That might be what they consider 'attempting to reunite children with their families.'

But my guess is that the authorities don't even do that; they focus on taking children into the system, not in helping them out of it. I think Annie's comments to me were genuine. For whatever reason, she wanted me to know what little she thought she knew.

But Mr Wilson was thorough and meticulous in his job of supervising my welfare. He seemed to care about me and my best interests. I have to believe that it was policy to keep me apart from my sister, to hide her from me. So, for 42 years, the authorities achieved their rather unhelpful objective: producing a proper orphan and another success story of a child in care who would hopefully grow to be a responsible adult.

And so, the coming weeks would represent a new beginning as my relationship with Jean took shape. Impromptu visits, phone calls, birthdays. We were building a relationship from scratch which should have been established decades ago. It was like jumping onto a bus that's already moving at full speed, rather than boarding at the beginning when we could've had time to take our seats and settle in. Some small details had to be dealt with sensitively like choosing greeting cards that didn't reference happy memories of our past life together. We didn't have any memories of each other.

Over cups of tea and sandwiches, we re-lived our experiences, filling in gaps for each other. I was keen to share my memories of our mother and the warmth and kindness she showed me in our few short years together. Until the day she left me, I had loved my time with Mother and wanted to convey this to Jean. She didn't have such a fortunate experience to share. She had been abandoned a few months after she was born and taken into care from the start of her life. It saddened me to hear another case of Mother abandoning her children. I couldn't understand her actions, and although I felt protective towards Mother, how could I defend her to Jean? Our different experiences of our mother had to be taken at face value by each of us. Then there was Roy and the mysterious twins. Hopefully Jean could fill in the missing gaps.

§§§

During these visits, Jean and Alan would produce boxes of photographs of their wedding day and from various stages of their lives. They had been a very photogenic couple, Jean with her blonde hair and film-star looks. The backgrounds of the photographs were often familiar to me. I was amazed to find that their wedding took place at St Christopher's Church in Speke. I had attended Speke Comprehensive school, directly opposite that church. The reception was held in the function room above the Childe of Hale pub, a place I had frequented as my 'local' in my late teenage years. Numerous other photos had Speke connections to places I was familiar with. We had lived virtually parallel lives, albeit at different times. There were so many places as familiar to me as they were to Jean and Alan.

Alan had lived in Speke prior to meeting Jean, and after they met, the couple had set up home less than a ten-minute walk from where I was living with the Foys.

It was an example of how close we had been without ever knowing of each other's presence. But there had been events and opportunities which could have brought us together far sooner.

I had suggested to Jean that she write to Social Services, as I had done since they would likely have information on her file that she would be entitled to. She did this, and soon after she received her file. Within the package was an old letter. The letter had been addressed to Jean but had been retained by the authorities. It was a letter from our father, Charles Williams, handwritten and dated April 1957. A photograph was enclosed. He stated that he had been attempting to meet her, waiting unsuccessfully outside Evan's Medical in Speke where she worked, trying to catch a glimpse of her as the workers streamed out in the evening. In the letter he invited her to visit him, providing his address on Falkner Street. But Social Services kept the letter. They didn't forward it to her, and it remained on file leaving Jean, now 60 years old, completely unaware that her father had been trying to contact her all those years ago.

The included photo was of Charles Williams at a party or some sort of social event. There were many other people in the picture, so he had rather pathetically put a cross next to his image so that Jean could identify him.

The letter had been his first and only known attempt to contact his daughter. They never met. The decision by Social Services to withhold the letter impacted my future, also. When he wrote to Jean, Mother would have been six-months pregnant with me. It was possible that this was the reason he wanted to meet Jean: to inform her of my imminent arrival.

But the letter didn't move from some social services filing cabinet until Jean requested her file 42 years later. Had it been delivered when it should have been, how differently things may have turned out.

Another unbelievable coincidence featured Sonia, Joey Foy's daughter, in the next near miss between my sister and me. Joey had been married previously, but sadly his first wife had passed away. He had gone on to marry Annie.

Joey's story had itself been a rather sad tale. He and his previous wife had three daughters and three sons. Joey was a dock worker and following the death of his wife had been unable to cope trying to balance the long hard days of dock work with supporting the needs of so many young children. He was forced to place them in care. Sonia had been placed in Fazakerley Cottage Homes.

Two of his sons lived in and around London and, so his daughters visited most often. Sonia would show up with her children every few weeks on Sundays, and they would stay for the afternoon. She would state that she was going to call round to see her friend before she headed home. No one ever knew who the 'friend' was, and it was never discussed. After I discovered my sister, Jean notified the local newspaper of our story, and they ran an article about our unlikely reunion. There was a photograph of Jean and me and an article on our story. The day after the article was published my phone rang.

'Ron, I got your number from the Liverpool Echo, remember me? It's Sonia.'

'Yes, of course, I remember you!'

'You don't know Jean Reay!'

'Of course, I do. At least I do now,' I responded. 'As you will have read, Jean is my sister.'

Sonia reminded me of the times she would visit her father all those years ago and tell us that she was going to call round to see her friend while she was in the area. 'The friend I used to visit,' stated Sonia, 'was Jean'.

Both had spent time in Fazakerley Cottage Homes together and had become close friends, but there had never been any reason for Sonia to make the link between Jean and me. Jean wasn't aware of me, and I wasn't aware of her. There wasn't anything to link the fact that Sonia was moving between my home and my sister's. But that was exactly what she was doing.

My relationship with Jean and Alan would open more doors that would further embed me into my family. Through Jean, I would go on to meet my half-brother, Roy. He was the only sibling I had been aware of as a child. Mother had told me that he was living in Canada, but this wasn't the case. It had been her justification for him not being around. Jean explained that Roy, too, had been abandoned by Mother at an early age and had been placed in care at Fazakerley Cottage Homes in Liverpool. Following a visit to the home from Mother, the siblings had been made aware of their relationship, so Roy and Jean had enjoyed much of their time at the home as brother and sister. Then Roy was taken from Fazakerley to be adopted. Jean wasn't informed that Roy had been removed and had been deeply upset to find that he had been taken from her.

In later years Roy would take up a career in the merchant navy, marrying and living on the Wirral. Although Jean and Roy hadn't been in constant contact, Jean suggested that I should meet him, and she arranged for us both to visit him at his home in Moreton.

Entering his home for the first time, Jean and I were greeted by Margaret, his wife. She was a loud woman, a real character who was warm and welcoming. Margaret had made a considerable effort in preparation for our visit. The table in the living room was filled with sandwiches and cakes.

The room was filled with people, too – family and friends of Margaret and Roy. It was a party atmosphere. Then I saw Roy. He didn't look how I expected. Track-suited, small and thin, this wasn't a well man. As I shook hands and greeted him, he didn't respond coherently. Margaret informed me that he had suffered a series of strokes, leaving him barely able to speak.

I sat beside him on the couch, looking into his face and searching for the visual likenesses and expressions that would link him to Mother. Roy didn't resemble Jean or me. He had come from a different father, and I didn't know who that father was. But the link to Mother was apparent. His 'sad-eyed' smile and gentle manners unquestionably belonged to her. We sat together. Although his speech was garbled and unintelligible, we found a way to chat without the need for his response to matter. *This is all too late*, I thought. *I'll never know the real Roy, my brother as he was.* It crossed my mind, 'Ron and Roy.' That would've sounded good as we introduced ourselves. It was ironic that Mother had given us similar names, but we would never share our experiences as family. As we muddled along, I was certain that he understood who I was, despite his inability to tell me so. Roy had experienced the unexpected and sudden loss of a son. Margaret told me that he was devastated. And this was probably a contributing factor to his illness.

Roy's home was often a busy place, and I couldn't help feeling that I was imposing when visiting him. Therefore, I limited my visits to Christmas time. I regret that I didn't see him more often. My visits to Roy exposed one of the real difficulties of meeting family later in life. I found it so difficult to 'calibrate' the relationship. When do you phone, and when do you visit? How often? For how long? Where is the line between being a bother and being a brother? I wrestled with trying to find the balance. The initial over-reaction of visiting and phoning too often was inevitably followed by a lessening of communications as things found a level. But I was never certain how to get (or if I got) the balance right. Phoning Roy wasn't really an option. I had to visit for our interaction to be meaningful.

During the early years of the 'noughties' (2000s), I became less inclined to make family visits. I was experiencing problems in my personal life. My wife and I were having difficulties that lead us to separate in late 2004. This was unchartered, turbulent territory. Whilst my wife and I knew it was time to part, our concern was to ensure that any emotional damage to our children was minimised. I had to focus on my girls.

In the time leading up to our separation and subsequent divorce, I didn't visit my family, not wanting to burden them with the negativity occurring in my own life. I, therefore, lost touch with Roy, and the break in my visits made it difficult to re-establish the connection. When some years later I finally called to the house, I discovered that both Roy and Margaret had passed away. However, much circumstance had played its part, I hadn't cultivated my relationship with him to the extent that I could have, and I would always feel that I should have spent more time with him. That said, I was glad that I had at least been given the opportunity to know Roy.

Jean had become the catalyst for connecting me with my blood family. In the same way that I was able to enlighten her about my experiences with Mother, she, in turn, had knowledge of other relatives. When I asked Jean if she knew anything about the two 'half-Chinese twins' that the Social Services report referred to, she recalled a visit to Mother when she was about twelve-years-old. Jean was at the home in Fazakerley at the time. She said, 'Mother was living with a Chinese seafarer. When I got there, she let me see and hold these darling newly born twins.'

Although she couldn't recall either the address of the property or the names of the children, she remembered the father, a kind Chinese man called Ah Moy. This was the first evidence of Mother's tangled relationships. I hadn't yet been born, and I, like Jean, would be born to another man: Charles Williams.

Jean's recollection wasn't enough information to begin a mission to find them, just a tantalising glimpse into the fact that they existed and a possibility to gauge their ages. But I needed names, a problem complicated by their Chinese father. Did they have Chinese or English names? Did they live somewhere around Speke or in China or somewhere else in the East or West? I hoped that there would be other clues yet to be revealed.

Jean told me about Uncle Jim, our mother's brother, who I had not heard of. She gave me his address and phone number. He and his wife, Jess, lived in Maghull on the outskirts of Liverpool. I dithered for some weeks before deciding to make contact. After more of my trademark shilly-shallying, I phoned and arranged to visit them at their home. I found the most loving, caring and delightful couple. Committed Baptists, Uncle Jim and Aunt Jess made me welcome from the start. They would go on to become an important part of my life, further connecting me with my family and giving me a sense of pride to be a Clark. Uncle Jim brought my mother's face back into my memory. He resembled her both in looks and through his mellow manner.

Uncle Jim took my knowledge of the family history to another level. He had spent many years researching the family tree and had traced the Clark family records back to the eighteenth century. His research had led him to Cumbria, where he had established that our ancestors lived in the small villages of Parton and Moresby, near the port of Whitehaven. One member of the family, William Clark, born in Parton in 1831, had travelled to Liverpool to make his living at sea. In 1857 he married local girl Mary Ann Harding. They settled in the city and brought five little Clarks into the world, thereby establishing the 'Liverpool Branch' of the family.

Uncle Jim and Aunt Jess had one daughter, Lynda. She, too, was interested in family history matters. Lynda's knowledge of ancestry software was instrumental to the events that were yet to unfold.

Go on Dad...Knock!

The Secret of the Rhubarb Tree

*It's hard sometimes to understand why people do the
things they do*

*'We should not judge.' Some people say and yet we do,
we often do...*

*So when a brother does not know the sister that he has
not met*

*And he in turn could live and die not knowing of this
secret yet,*

*There must be some good reason why. There must be
ways to justify,*

*There must be things that make it right to hold from one
the other's sight.*

*Like Christmastime, like weddings missed, like
birthdays and like getting pissed*

*But don't tell one about the other, you know what she
was like, 'that mother...'*

*So you might say 'I do not know about the boy, then he
will grow*

*To never be aware of you, nor you of him, that's
what we'll do'.*

*Then say 'I did not know of him and he in turn
didn't know me'.*

*But one day everyone will learn the secret of the
rhubarb tree.*

Go on Dad...Knock!

Chapter Eight: The Rhubarb Tree

Violet was one of Mother's three sisters. My first encounter with her was brief but memorable. Long ago she lived in a pre-fabricated house on the outskirts of Liverpool on the Belle Vale housing estate.

One day Mother took me on a visit to Violet. As a little boy, I was bored with their adult conversation, so I wandered out to play in the neat garden at the rear of the little pre-fab. Violet's husband, Norman, pointed out the various flowers that were growing there. He made it seem like a game; it was fun.

Then to my amazement, he said, 'And this one is rhubarb'.

'Rhubarb? But rhubarb is food!' I exclaimed, unable to understand the link between a plant and

135

something that appeared on my plate at school dinner time.

'Yes, but look, it grows in the ground,' Norman explained, pulling some sticks of rhubarb for me to see. It really did look like rhubarb.

I ran into the house and shouted, 'Mother, Auntie Violet has a rhubarb tree!' Everyone laughed and enjoyed the moment.

Thirty-six years later, Auntie Violet's name was once again coming into focus. My conversations with Jean and Uncle Jim inevitably covered areas where we had common ground. Both Jean and Jim were in touch with Violet, who had moved to the Isle of Man years earlier. She had been a successful businesswoman in her time and was now enjoying her retirement. Jean and Jim both questioned whether she knew anything about me. They asked her. She said that she didn't know who I was. When Jean put this to me, I told her to remind Violet of the special moment that we had shared so many years ago.

'Ask her about the rhubarb tree'.

Next time Jean spoke to Violet, she told her what I had said about Violet's rhubarb plants. She could no longer deny it. Violet could no longer claim ignorance of me to Jean. She had chosen not to pass on her knowledge of me to my siblings. In her opinion, I had been one child too many, and she had airbrushed me out of her thoughts. Violet had been a good woman. She had done her best to look after Roy following Mother's desertion while bringing up a family of her own. She had a good relationship with Jean and with Uncle Jim. But I think that news of the twins, then me, had made her feel that enough is enough. She no longer wanted to be involved in Mother's growing list of deserted off-springs.

So, when in 2001, I found myself on the Isle of Man heading to a business meeting with some potential new customers, the last thing I expected was that I would be having a meeting with Violet.

During my stay, I took a stroll along the main street in Douglas and noticed a fishmonger selling Manx kippers. I recalled that Jean and Alan had said they loved Manx kippers, so I called Jean to explain where I was and to offer to bring her some home. When we spoke, she threw a curveball that I wasn't expecting.

'Why not visit Aunt Violet?' she asked.

I was intrigued.

Jean told me to hang up and await her call. Moments later my mobile phone rang. It was Jean.

'I've called Violet. She'd love to see you.'

I was surprised that Violet was positive about seeing me. I had become the reason for some frostiness in her relationship with both Jean and Uncle Jim. But Violet was now an old lady; it wasn't a time for recriminations over what might have been. What had happened in the past had happened. Now that Jean had made a visit to Violet possible, I was quite excited at the prospect of meeting her.

Driving up to Governors Hill, an area on the outskirts of Douglas, I once again felt the onset of dry mouth and sweaty palms that was becoming my family–finding trademark. Violet greeted me at the door. I saw the family connection straightaway. She was an elderly woman who had wisdom etched on her face – a woman who had lived. She smiled, we embraced, and she ushered me into her smart apartment.

There was none of the awkwardness that I had anticipated, and I played my part in keeping it that way. I didn't question her reasoning for 'keeping quiet about me,' and I was aware that she didn't speak ill of Mother. In fact, our conversation flowed easily. She had daughters and grandchildren living on the Island. We spoke at length about them and my own family in Liverpool. I thoroughly enjoyed her company, as I believe she enjoyed mine. I wondered if she may have harboured pre-conceived ideas about the type of person I might be, only to find that I wasn't that person at all. When the time came to leave, we embraced. As I waved her goodbye, I noticed that she was tearful. Perhaps I reminded her of Mother as much as Violet reminded me of her.

Violet passed away a couple of years later. I was glad that I had a memory of her to keep. As for my business meetings, they weren't as gratifying. Despite calling on several potential clients on the Island, I didn't get a scrap of business. Absolutely nothing. But I had connected with my Isle of Man family, making my visit to the Island priceless.

§§§

Winding forward to 2014, the Beatles managed to sum up how I felt, 'My life had changed in, oh, so many ways!' I had a new lady in my life, Ann, whom I had met in 2005, whilst simply minding my own business watching a Liverpool football game at Anfield.

I turned to the woman in the seat next to mine, shouting, 'That was a great goal!' Mind you, this was after leaping out of my seat when Steven Gerard blasted the winner into the net. I didn't realise at the time, but *I* would score at that game, too. Ann was the little lady in the adjacent seat at the next game I attended. We had 'hit it off,' and I bravely asked her to meet me for a drink at a local pub.

I had decided that I was going to be a single man for the rest of my life after my first marriage failed, but I hadn't counted on meeting Ann. By 2013 we had married, moved into a new home in North Liverpool, and I had acquired three 'new' step-kids.

Warren, Katy and Hayley were the new additions to add to my own existing 'collection,' of children: Laura and Amanda. All of them had, to my great joy, developed good relationships with each other as 'steppies.'

Now it was summertime, and there were choices to make.

'Buxton or Douglas, Ann?'

After the hectic year we had spent previously, we needed a nice weekend break. Ann hadn't been to the Isle of Man before, and I suggested that a little boat trip would feel more like a proper holiday.

I also pointed out that it might be nice to take a good book since the island's capital, Douglas, may no longer be the tourist trap it had been famous for in bygone years. Its tourism industry had been diminished in exchange for a more lucrative role as a centre for banking and finance. We agreed that a long weekend in Douglas felt right.

We boarded the 'Manaman' on a bright–if windy – Saturday morning all set for a peaceful break. The catamaran made its way down the river Mersey and throttled up, accelerating towards Liverpool Bay. In no time, the calm of the river transformed into the raging Irish sea. Not just 'choppy' but terrifying.

'Why didn't you just take me to Buxton?' Ann screamed, clinging to her seat and holding me personally responsible. It was bad. When the swell became ruthless, the ceiling above us rattled loudly as if it was going to fall in. I tried to manage a just-another-fun-adventure look so as not to exacerbate Ann's stormy mood and ghost-like pallor. But my forced, stiff smiles and overly-emphasised winks did nothing to hide my misgivings. Neither did my white-knuckled clinging to whatever might save us from going down with the ship. Despite the drama of the voyage, we made it to Douglas, and prepared for our relaxing weekend.

We took a stroll down the main road through Douglas. As we did, I saw the fishmongers and recalled that they triggered my call to Jean some years earlier. I explained the story to Ann.

'Ring her again! She may want you to take her kippers just like last time.'

So I did.

Just as last time, Jean threw me a curveball. I got the order for kippers, but Jean also suggested that I look up Violet's daughters, Doreen and Alma.

Jean explained that they ran a hairdressing salon somewhere in Douglas and that the salon may now be owned by Doreen's daughters. This presented a challenge. When you're male, middle-aged and bald, there's no place on earth further from your comfort zone than a hairdressing salon. Did I want to walk into one of those places asking questions? No.

I discussed Jean's suggestion with Ann, who offered to solve the problem for me.

We proceeded along the shopping street, and suddenly Ann was on a mission. She spotted a hairdressing salon and disappeared inside. Moments later she re-appeared.

'Nope, it's not that one,' she said.

Then she spotted another one further along the street. 'No, it's not this one either,' she said. 'But now I know where it is!'

The people in the second salon had recognised the names. They told Ann where to find the hairdressing salon that they believed was the one owned by Violet's family.

'Salon Three' was a little further along the road, above a men's clothing shop. We entered and climbed the stairs to the reception. We were greeted by a friendly young lady. I was clearly outside my element. Ann pushed forward and took the lead.

'We're looking for relatives of Violet, her daughters. They're relatives of Ron's,' Ann explained. The girl disappeared into an office, and another young lady appeared.

'I'm Yvonne,' she explained. Ann pointed out my relationship as her mother's cousin.

'Oh, my God! I need to phone Mum. Please sit down!' She made a hurried phone call and asked us to wait at the coffee shop around the corner from the salon.

As we waited, a lady crossed the road towards us. Her appearance was immediately familiar. She looked like Jean. She glanced around the coffee shop until we made eye contact. There stood Violet's daughter and my newly-found cousin, Doreen. We hugged and introduced ourselves and as we did another car pulled up. In walked Alma. We greeted her. More cars and more family arrived.

In no time we were surrounded by a dozen or so new-found family members who had all rushed down to the coffee shop to greet us. As we sat drinking and getting to know each other, I was once again aware of the feeling that I had experienced before: familiarity with people who had been complete strangers moments earlier. We spent the whole weekend meeting up and being chaperoned around the island during an unexpected special weekend we wouldn't forget. I reflected on how easy it would have been to have viewed Violet through a negative lens and held a bitter grudge. Having met her, and now her off-springs, I simply felt blessed that I was a small part of this wonderful, and for me, ever-growing family.

Go on Dad...Knock!

Chapter Nine: Wong or Yong

Jean had largely enjoyed her childhood in care at Fazakerley Cottage Homes. In later life she helped organise reunions for the ex-residents, recalling her times there with fondness. She had been assisting a local newspaper which was running a feature on the Cottage Homes. During a conversation with a journalist, Jean happened to mention the story of how I had contacted her, and how she had not previously known of my existence. When the story finally appeared in the newspaper, it had been made into two features: history about the Cottage Homes and the story of Jean being discovered by her brother. The article appeared in the *Liverpool Echo* on 23 July 2014.

The day after the story appeared in the paper, Jean called me up.

'I've had a call,' she said, 'from Kim.'

'That's great! Who's Kim?' I didn't know if she was someone new or if I had somehow forgotten how she was connected to my growing web of family connections.

'She's Sandra's daughter,' explained Jean.

'Sandra?' I was truly lost. When I was an orphan, I longed for family. Now that I had this ever-expanding family, I couldn't remember them all!

'Yes, Sandra, our Auntie Lily's daughter, she remembers you from your childhood when you used to visit Auntie Lily with our Mum. She remembers you. Kim is *her* daughter calling me!'

'Oh.' It was finally sinking in.

'She's seen the article in the newspaper and wants to meet you'.

Sandra had seen the newspaper article and concluded that I must be the same 'Ronnie' that she remembered from the past, her Auntie Betty's son.

Kim took up the case. Following some research, she had managed to find Jean's number and contact her. She asked Jean to forward her number to me. I wasn't the only one with the urge to connect with family.

I called Kim.

'I know all about Auntie Betty,' Kim explained. 'My mum loved her and has told me so many stories about her.'

It was lovely to hear someone speaking about Mother and saying such positive things about her. Kim and Cousin Sandra wanted to meet me, and so we arranged for them to call at my home a few days later.

It was a warm and sunny August day when the doorbell sounded. There stood Sandra and Kim. Sandra was no longer the young girl of my childhood, but her face was immediately familiar. Following a group hug, Kim marched through to the kitchen to make tea for us all.

We were soon reminiscing about Auntie Lily, Mother and the happy times when she, 'Auntie Betty,' and I would go out together. Her recall of the past seemed to be very good, and so I asked Sandra if she knew anything about the twins.

'So far,' I explained, 'all I know is that they were twins and that they were half-Chinese.' I told Sandra and Kim that I had essentially given up on the idea that I'd ever find them. 'For all I know they could be in China, and I've been unable to trace their names'.

I told Sandra how my daughters had been on my case for some time to 'Find the Twins.' They would often bring up the subject anytime family matters were discussed. 'Find the Twins dad. Find the Twins.' They thought that because I had managed to find Jean, I could simply decide to find someone else and they would pop-up to order!

Sandra paused for a moment, deep in thought.

'Wong.' She said suddenly. 'Mr Wong. That was the father's name'.

I was taken aback by this. Although I had put the question to Sandra, I had hardly expected her to come back with anything. At last, this could be the clue I needed.

Our afternoon continued with the promise that we would keep in touch. I was thrilled to have met Sandra again after so many years. I was grateful to Kim for following her instincts and bringing us together. In doing so, she had delivered an important clue that could help me find the twins.

Jean had told me previously that she had a faint recollection of seeing the twins when she was very young, but that was it. Her memory didn't stretch to recalling them by name. Suddenly, my long-lost cousin, Sandra, appeared to have brought us something of a breakthrough.

I told Laura and Amanda that we had news about the twins and that my meeting with Sandra had revealed a possible name. 'Wong.' Half-joking, we talked about the jewellers in Liverpool, 'Wong's.' 'You never know Dad,' said Amanda, 'it could be them...'

Laura decided to take matters into her own hands, making a call to the jewellers and explaining the story. Mr Wong proved to be a gentleman, but he didn't have a twin. However, he promised her he would give her a great deal on a watch if she ever decided to call into the shop!

The next time I visited Jean, I explained to her about my meeting with Sandra and Kim. I told her that I had discussed the twins, and they had come up with a name. I told her, 'It's Wong, Jean, that's the father's name'.

'No!' Jean replied. 'It's YONG!'

The name, remembered slightly inaccurately by Sandra, had nonetheless triggered a distant memory in Jean. 'It's YONG! I'm sure of it.'

A shiver ran down my spine as I realised the importance of the moment. Jean had remembered the twins' father's first name, 'Ah Moy.' Now it all came together thanks to the prompt from Sandra.

'Ah Moy YONG!'

Thanking Jean, I drove home thinking over the next move. I knew someone who could help me with this. Uncle Jim's daughter, Lynda, had an account with Ancestry.com. When we had met previously, my new-found cousin had shown a great deal of interest in family matters. She enjoyed hearing of my adventures finding Jean and our Isle of Man family. The day after learning about Ah Moy Yong, I called Lynda and explained about Sandra's visit, that we had some newly-acquired information on the twins and enlisted her help. In no time Lynda and I were working on the project, researching the Yong name to see where it led. I also downloaded a free, trial version of Ancestry, believing that we might crack this within fourteen days. This would prove to be a sound financial decision. Whilst we didn't know exactly when the twins were born, Jean's vague memory of seeing them when they were tiny babies became relevant. She had told us that she was about twelve-years-old at the time, making the target search year around 1950. We, therefore, had the possibility of making a rough calculation of their ages. We set out some parameters based on Jean's age for the likely birth years of the twins and trawled through the data on Ancestry.

I was concerned that the name 'Yong' could be a Chinese equivalent of Smith or Jones in the UK, but it didn't matter because Lynda got there first. And she was a brilliant researcher!

She called me to say that she'd found a birth entry for December 1950, for a 'Raymond Frederick Clark or Yong,' and I subsequently found the matching entry for one 'Carol Irene Clark or Yong,' dated the same.

It was displayed in the register as 'Clark or Yong,' as though the parents couldn't make up their minds, or maybe there had been some doubt which name to use if it had been Social Services, rather than the parents, registering the births.

Either way, it was a big help to us because the 'double-barrelled' surname entry meant there could be absolutely no doubt that we had found the twins!

They had western names after all. Suddenly these two people were beginning to look real. There was a feeling of momentum. This was 2015, and I realised that there might be much quicker ways of locating people than there had been sixteen years ago when I had found Jean.

I was never a natural fan of Facebook; I struggled to come to terms with people who uploaded photos of their lunch or aired their grievances with others for all to see. Nonetheless, semi-reluctantly, I signed up, and in no time, I was networking again with various old friends and acquaintances. My old school friend, Doug in Australia, had wisely pointed out to me that he had a thousand friends on Facebook, but no-one would help him when he was moving house. His story illustrated that Facebook popularity wasn't always the same as genuine popularity. But I hadn't signed up to make new friends or engage in trivia. My singular aim in using this media was to find the twins.

Not wanting to rely on Facebook alone, I started searching combinations of names on Google; it was a long-shot but a shot, nonetheless. Both the twins had middle names, a big help in narrowing down possibilities.

It wasn't long before I found what seemed to be a match, at least for one of them. A local newspaper contained an article that involved someone with my brother Raymond's name and who was of a similar age. But he was in the newspaper because had been sent to prison for robbing his customers of thousands of pounds. My heart sunk.

Whilst the specifics of the crime are probably best left untold, for quite a while I convinced myself that he was, indeed, my long-lost brother. The possibility of my quest leading me to a prison had never entered my mind, and I was no longer certain that my journey had any more mileage in it. After some thought, I decided to press forward with the hope that this criminal wasn't my Raymond. It was wrong to stop now, and anyway I still had to find Irene, Raymond's twin and my sister.

Lynda and I had found evidence of a marriage on Ancestry between 'Carole Irene Clark' and a man called Smith. During my trawling on Google, I found further threads on a Smith family website of an individual trying to contact Carole Irene Smith and her husband. It gave details of an address in Liverpool. It also provided their children's names. Using these, I trawled Facebook until I found the likely profile of a woman, now called Irene (not Carole). She looked part Asian.

I sent a message. No reply.

I searched the details of her contacts. There were two young men whose last name was Clark. Both looked part Chinese. Furthermore, there appeared to be evidence that they were twins. Could they be Raymond's sons? I searched their contacts and found that one had been married recently. A thought crossed my mind, *search his contacts and find his wife.* I found her. Sure enough, her Facebook page contained multiple wedding photos. She was clearly of South East Asian appearance. I looked for a photograph of the entire family. I found it. Standing alongside my suspected potential nephew was an adult male of Chinese appearance. A warm feeling immediately bonded me to the image.

'Ann, I think I've got a picture of Raymond, here on Facebook.' Ann took one look at it and agreed I was possibly onto something. There was, however, no reference to him personally, and he didn't have a Facebook profile. But he also wasn't wearing handcuffs, nor was he standing behind bars, so the excitement of these fast-moving events also came with some relief! If this was indeed Raymond, then he wasn't the criminal from my previous search. The wedding photos had clearly not been taken in the UK. There was a tropical flavour to the scenes, and the men, extremely smartly dressed, were also dressed for the heat in predominantly white clothing. I had learned that the bride was Indonesian. The man I had singled out for further attention was also extremely smart, and my instinct told me he was a businessman. An idea popped into my head.

Because I run my own small business, I had been invited by some of my customers and suppliers to connect online to the business app, LinkedIn.

I barely ever used it but understood it was a sort of Facebook for business, a networking tool. I knew that one of its functions was to find other business contacts to connect with them. The man we saw looked very business-like. Maybe LinkedIn could help me connect with him.

On LinkedIn, I typed in Raymond F. Clark. There before me was a profile. This man ran a hotel group in Bali, Indonesia. He had multiple qualifications in hotel management. He was also a highly qualified chef, and as I scrolled down through the various locations he had worked and trained, the list ascended backwards from present day, Bali, Indonesia, Sandals Jamaica, Bournemouth UK, then... *'Trained at Colquitt Street Catering College, Liverpool.'*

I fumbled for the telephone, I needed to call Lynda. We had found Raymond.

Chapter Ten: Find the Twins

Nosing through the website for 'The Samaya' in Seminyak, Bali, the description is of 'A Five-Star hotel, offering modern villas with private pools in a resort offering 24-hour butler services with spa and restaurant.' The site goes on to depict blissful scenes of guests dining at the hotel's beachfront restaurant, silhouetted against a magnificent golden sunset.

Pictures of hotel staff bedecked in colourful Indonesian costume could be seen clasping hands and bowing politely as they greeted arriving guests in a paradise setting oozing charm and class. Clicking through the photo gallery, 'The Samaya' looked like heaven on earth.

On the front page of the website, there's a welcoming introduction from the hotel's General Manager, Raymond Clark. FIH, CHA, CHP, Cert. Ed. The note finished with his handwritten signature, which appeared to have a capital 'F' after 'Raymond,' a further positive indication given that Lynda and I had found the birth entry for Raymond 'Frederick' Clark.

This had to be Raymond, and I had to decide what to do next. I had no idea what type of personality Raymond was, we clearly had made our lives in very different environments, and it was probable that Raymond knew nothing about me. I decided to locate the hotel and try to contact Raymond via email. I could only find a generic email for 'The Samaya,' so I formulated a simple email that didn't reveal the personal nature of the message, not knowing who would open it.

'Dear Mr Clark, I wonder if you would be kind enough to call me on my (UK) phone, as I would like to have a discussion with you, Yours Faithfully Ron Clark.'

I sent the email late that evening. When I awoke next morning, I had a return email on my mobile phone from 'The Samaya.'

'Ron, I will call you at 8:30 am UK time. We are eight hours ahead here in Bali, Raymond.'

The reply seemed so informal. I wondered what he thought when he saw 'Ron Clark' as the signature on the email. Did he have any idea that I might be a long-lost family member?

It was 7:00 am, and as I rose for work, I was trying to suppress my nervousness. I knew that the phone would soon ring. I tried to compose my side of the conversation before it happened. At exactly 8:30, my phone rang. An international number. Raymond.

'Hello, this is Raymond. It's Ron?'

'Yes, it is. Hello, how are you? Thank you for calling me'.

'No problem, I saw that you are in the UK. Like I said in my email, we are eight hours ahead of you here, so we need to be careful when we call people!'

'Thank you. I hope you don't mind what I'm going to tell you. It's absolutely nothing to worry about, but you may have noticed my name on the email I sent you...'

'Yes, it's very similar to mine, are you going to tell me that we are family?'

'Yes, Ray, I am. You're my brother'.

'Jesus!' He paused before continuing. 'You know, Ron, we always knew there was family, but we could never get to the bottom of it. Irene tried a few times when I was over in the UK with her, but we couldn't get anywhere. I certainly didn't know about you!'

Raymond was obviously taken aback, but he was easy to talk to.

Our conversation wasn't awkward – quite the opposite. We formed an instant connection. He explained that he had always known about a Liverpool family connection, but that was all he knew. He certainly had no idea that he had siblings. I told him how difficult it had been to find the evidence that had finally led me to make this call.

His knowledge of his family was limited to his twin, Irene. We conversed as though we had known each other for a lifetime. I told him about Jean and Roy. As our conversation progressed, Raymond's family was growing. He, in turn, told me about Irene, who was living in the UK in Wigan, a short hop down the motorway from my Liverpool home. Despite the distance between Raymond and Irene, they were in constant touch with each other.

Raymond explained how he and Irene had often discussed the family they knew so little about. Irene had made previous attempts to locate family without success. Some years ago, she managed to locate one of her aunts, but she didn't get a good reception. Was her rejection because she was Mother's daughter or (worse still) because she was mixed-race and a victim of prejudice from the aunt? This had an obvious and understandable effect on Irene's view of the family she knew so little of and did little to encourage her to continue to search.

§§§

Raymond and Irene, therefore, decided that the odds were against them finding any members of their family and decided to stop trying. I explained to Raymond that I also had been completely unaware of my siblings (except for Roy) for most of my life. Before meeting Jean, I didn't know the whereabouts of Roy. Now here I was at 58 years old talking to Ray for the first time.

It dawned on us that Mother had been playful in her choice of names for her sons.

Roy, Ray and Ron.

We spoke for maybe an hour in an easy conversation. Raymond seemed happy and keen to be putting the missing parts of the family jigsaw puzzle together. Despite his lofty position as General Manager of a millionaire's paradise, he was earthy and grounded. Our mutual sense of humour had connected as we laughed our way through our first-ever conversation.

I told Ann afterwards that I felt Ray and I were going to have some fun in the future. With that came the unspoken sadness of the times we had missed out on in the past.

Raymond had given me a phone number for Irene and informed me that he would be in London on business during November. We agreed that we would meet up when he came over, and we said our goodbyes. I hung up feeling drained by a mixture of euphoria and sadness. Ann had overheard our conversation and said what I had been thinking.

'So much lost time.'

I waited until later that day before calling Irene. I rang the number, and a young lady answered the phone. She had excitement in her voice when I asked for Irene. I guessed Raymond had already spoken to her in preparation for my call.

I had been speaking with Irene's daughter Katherine.

Minutes later I was talking to Irene, introducing myself yet again to a 'new' sibling. Irene reiterated Raymond's earlier story of how she had tried to find her relatives and failed, and I wanted to reassure her that I was delighted to have found them both. I wanted to visit her as soon as possible. In our conversation, I told her that my big regret was that I didn't have a picture of our Mother. I had never been able to show my girls what she looked like.

'I've got one,' Irene replied. 'It's on my wall. Every morning I say good morning to her, and goodnight in the evenings. You can copy it. Then you will have one too.' We arranged a meet.

A couple of days later I was off to Wigan. As I turned into the little terraced street and pulled up outside Irene's house, I was again a mess of nerves, apprehension and excitement.

Knock, knock. Pause.

There stood Irene. In her face, I saw her history. The deep-set, kindly eyes of Mother set against the slightly oriental features from her Chinese father, Ah Moy Yong. As I thrust a bouquet of flowers into her hand, we hugged and stared. I simply said, 'Hiya, Sis.'

Irene replied, 'Hi, Brother'.

I learned that life hadn't always been kind to Irene. I wanted her to know that if she had felt disenfranchised from her family, then it had been no different for me. I, too, had been brought up away from my blood relatives. I told her how I'd found family members one-by-one and finding my family had been a beautiful experience. I assured her these relatives would all be delighted to know that we had now found her. She wouldn't be rejected. Our family was finally becoming complete.

Irene rewarded me with a moment to treasure as she produced the picture that we had talked about on the phone. It was a framed picture of my mum. Once again, Mother's smiling face was there for me, and my family, to see.

§§§

It was November 2014, and Ray was coming to London! We had agreed to meet in the capital. As Ann and I journeyed down on the train, we speculated about how things might turn out. Ray and I had spoken on the telephone, but now we were off to meet him in person. I knew that our paths had taken us in different directions, me with my tiny little garage equipment business, Ray running two stunning hotels in Bali.

We had arranged to meet at the Holiday Inn near Euston, at 8 p.m. where Ann and I were staying. By happy coincidence, Ray's son, Colin, was in London for a wedding, flying in from his home in Singapore. His other son, Ian, had arranged to come up from Bournemouth to meet Ray in London. As we prepared in our hotel room, my nerves were shot. I had dealt with the acquisition of two elder sisters, but an elder brother was somehow a different dynamic. As we checked in to the Holiday Inn, a very pleasant receptionist asked what the occasion was that brought us to London. Ann explained I was an hour or so away from meeting my brother for the first time. The receptionist, visibly moved, arranged for a bottle of wine to be sent to our room with her compliments. It was a lovely touch and one which I began to make immediate use of before we made our way downstairs!

As 8:00 pm approached, I had sampled too much complimentary wine. Ann faffed around with her clothing and hair, showing her usual reluctance to conform to anything related to timekeeping. Eventually, we made our way down to Reception, sitting slightly huddled in a corner of the foyer. At 8 pm prompt, Ray and Ian marched purposefully in through the hotel entrance. We stood, walked over and embraced.

'Let's go find a pub,' Ray said, and off we went, 100 yards down the road, where we found a proper London pub, 'The Green Man.'

'Here's to our first beer together,' said Ray, as we all raised our glasses.

As we chatted away over our first meal together, our unfortunate waitress tripped and fell on her backside. She wasn't hurt, but our fish and chips went flying everywhere. She saw the funny side of it, and so did we; we all roared with laughter. *What a formidable pair we would have made if we'd known each other sooner,* I thought as we all laughed and joked through our first evening. Before we parted, Ray let us know that he was returning to the UK in a few months. That would be a good time for him to meet Jean. I decided to organise a get-together at a little corner pub, the Victoria, in Waterloo.

Following a quick call to the Isle of Man, Auntie Violet's daughters (Doreen and Alma) agreed immediately to be there, along with Uncle Jim's daughter (Lynda) and her husband (Dave), Auntie Lily's daughter (Sandra) and her daughter (Kim), my daughters (Laura and Amanda), my step-kids (Warren, Katy and Hayley), my sister and her husband (Jean and Alan), my other sister (Irene) and my brother Roy's daughter (Debbie). Along with Ann and me and other members of Ann's family, the gathering grew to maybe forty or so people.

On the arranged day and time, ever-prompt Ray walked into the Vic with his twin, Irene. The pub was packed with our new-found family.

'I believe you are my Brother.' Jean stood holding out her arms. 'I'm Jean. It's lovely to meet you.'

Irene stepped up. 'Hello, Jean. Hello, Sister!'

As they embraced, smiles and tears graced the faces of the people who had played their parts in bringing our family together. Witnessing the beautiful moment as the siblings met was breath-taking. The room was a happy celebration, not so much a reunion as a union since many of those in the room hadn't met previously.

§§§

Kim, meanwhile, had informed me that there were more people to discover. She was in touch with the Parr family, descendants of Mother's sister, Auntie Jane Parr. They were a big family. Kim suggested waiting until after the Victoria pub gathering to contact the Parrs, as we wanted to give Ray and Irene the chance to meet Jean. Good to her word, one day she pulled up outside my house with Margaret Parr, wife of Harry, Auntie Jane's son. Harry had sadly passed away a few years ago.

I learned that Harry had been a much-loved, larger-than-life character who had been very friendly with Mother. When Margaret opened her car door to meet me, I gave her a hug. She was tearful as she explained that she would have loved Harry to have been around for this meeting. We went off for a coffee and a chat. Before Margaret left, she invited Ann and me to her house in Kirkby the following week.

Arriving there, Ann and I were overwhelmed with the number of Parr relatives. There were loads of them, all wanting to meet Betty's long-lost son. Many of them were my second cousins (Harry and Margaret's children) and other second cousins from Harry's brother, Roy. Margaret beckoned Ann and me into the living room, asking the rest of the family to form a circle around us. Organiser, Mandy, had been filling flutes with champagne.

'Ron and Ann, would you please stand in the centre,' said Margaret.

'Would everyone please raise their glasses to Ron and Ann. We would like to welcome you back into the family'.

We raised our glasses, surrounded by this beautiful family. I caught sight of Kim, tears streaming down her cheeks, rushing out from the room. I'm sure she was overwhelmed by the moment and Margaret's heartfelt, welcoming speech.

Kim had organised meeting my Kirkby family. We both knew I had come to the end of my journey. But Kim also knew how far we had come: from my days in Kent Gardens, through the wilderness of having no family for many years, culminating in this beautiful and emotional day – the final link in the reconnection of our family.

* * *

One year later in 2016, Ray invited Ann and me to Bali. Bali! He was coming to the UK that August on business but had a couple of days to spare. He wanted us to accompany him back, with the bonus of spending a couple of days with Ray's son, our new-found nephew, Colin, in Singapore, before following on to Bali.

Ray wasn't finished giving me thrilling news. He pointed out that my long-held dream to visit my friends Doug and Angie Hesketh in Perth could become a reality, as Perth was a short three-hour flight from Bali. 'We could easily add a few days in Australia to our itinerary,' Ray said. 'Would you mind if my Daisy [his wife] and I join you and Ann?

We promise not to be *too much* of a bother." Ray winked and had that devilish smile that suddenly burst into laughter, a characteristic we both shared.

Ann looked at both of us, amazed. 'I can't tell which one of you is laughing. You both sound the same!'

Ann and I suggested that while Ray was in the UK, this would be another opportunity for everyone to meet up. This time the family gathering was going to be big. Everyone wanted to see the twins, and there was enthusiasm from all involved to see the family together. Newly-found sister, Irene, and her Wigan family would attend. Ray would travel from Heathrow to Bournemouth to link up with his sons, Ian and Rodney, and their families. His son, Colin, living in Singapore, was coming over too. Sister Jean and her husband Alan were coming with my nephew Alan and his wife, Kate. The many descendants of my Auntie Jane, the Parr family, who we had met at our big Kirkby welcome party, were also coming.

Uncle Jim's daughter, Lynda, who had been so helpful and involved during my research was coming along with her husband, Dave. Auntie Violet's descendants, Doreen and Alma, my recently-found cousins from the Isle of Man were flying over. Cousin Sandra (Auntie Lillie's daughter) and her daughter, Kim, who had provided the vital clue that ultimately led us to the twins were keen to attend, and Kim's son, Luke, wanted to be there, too; he was flying in from university in Budapest.

Touchingly, our departed brother Roy's daughter, Debbie, was coming along with her daughters. Lifelong brother, Steve (Foy), and his wife, Pauline, were invited and said they would be there. Last in the long list of attendees but first in my heart: my wife, Ann, my daughters, Laura and Amanda, and step-kids, Warren, Kate and Hayley.

With the addition of Ann's family, there would be upwards of 90 people in the room, and most of them related to each other; many would be meeting for the first time.

It was 20 August 2016, the day of the reunion/union, and it was heart-warming to look around and see my family together. Everyone was having a good time. I took a moment to sit in a corner and observe, finally realising where all my research, leg-work, stubbornness and luck had led. I thought about Mother, and how proud she would have been to have seen us all together.

The next week we were to fly to Heathrow to meet up with Ray again and begin our adventure to Bali. Ann hadn't flown long haul before. So, there was some trepidation about the trip. I tried my best to distract her with my charm, but that got old fast. Ann's a trooper, though, and the trip was as pleasant as any thirteen-hour-long flight could be.

Colin sent a taxi to collect us at Changi, and we spent a wonderful couple of days being shown the sights of Singapore. Ann doesn't like heights, so Colin arranged to take us to a special bar known as 'Altitude,' Singapore's highest bar on the roof of a skyscraper. We had a stunning (or staggering, depending on one's phobias) view overlooking the city. Ann came through it with flying colours after some initial 'words' with Colin. Despite this altitude miss-step, he was an amazing host. Our stay in Singapore made for a wonderful start to our South East Asian adventure that would lead us to Ray's home in Bali.

There were some surprises along the way. When travelling abroad (or anywhere), surprises are generally not welcome. These were.

The plane touched down at Ngurah Ria Airport, and we gathered our carry-on luggage from the overhead locker. As the plane door opened and we took our turn exiting the aircraft, we noticed a smartly dressed young man in the exit tube as we stepped through the door. He was holding up a card that read, 'Mr Ron and Mrs Ann Clark.'

'That's us,' I said, approaching the young man.

'Follow me,' he said. 'I'm going to get your luggage'.

As we followed him, he explained, 'You don't have to bother with the luggage carousel. Just wait here for one moment, please.' He led us to a small room and disappeared through a door. Minutes later, he emerged with our luggage. 'Now follow me,' he said. 'I'll take you to your transport. I work for the hotel.'

Ann and I looked at each other with our own versions of 'Wow!' silently etched on our faces.

I managed, 'You don't say.'

'Yes Sir, VIP service,' he explained.

We tried to straighten up and act like Very Important People.

As we walked towards the airport exit, we heard a shout from the floor above us. A camera flashed followed by the now-familiar roar of Ray's laugh. Waving from a balcony above us was Ray and Daisy, Ray's beautiful wife.

Our Bali adventure had begun.

The people carrier weaved its way through the crazy night traffic – a mess of scooters, mopeds and anything else on two wheels somehow managing to avoid each other. The driver seemed unperturbed by the chaos, and his calm demeanour was reassuring. We chatted about Singapore, and how well Ann had coped with the long flight. After about 30 minutes, the vehicle pulled into the hotel driveway. *Wow*, I thought, *this is some place. Ray manages a lot more than a hotel!* Not a huge hotel complex, this was a captivating resort in a picturesque setting, with a stepped frontage leading to an inviting lobby with mahogany beams and subtle lighting. Windows in the lobby neatly framed the scene beyond: palm trees and the pathway to the beachfront restaurant. It was a study in understated opulence.

Uniformed security guards scanned the underside of the vehicle then gave us clearance to pull in alongside the steps to the entrance of the hotel. There was a flurry of activity as the hotel staff, aware of the arriving vehicle, lined the steps. They were spectacularly dressed in traditional Bali costume. As we stepped out of the vehicle, two of the young women came forward to place garlands around our necks, as another came forward to present us with cocktails.

We made our way down to the beachside bar to enjoy a late drink. Along the way we laughed and joked with Ray and his wonderful staff. The days ahead would be our opportunity to get to know each other and to share our stories. I had a feeling of closure, that this was now *our* time. The waiter approached with a tray of drinks for the four of us. As we raised our glasses, I felt an overwhelming surge of emotion – an awareness that this was, indeed, journey's end.

And the start of a new beginning.

Just One Day

Some kids say they don't like their mam
Some kids don't like their dad
Some kids believe their childhood
Was the worst they've ever had
Some kids don't like their siblings
Some kids don't like their pet
Some kids don't like their grandparents
One day they may regret

Some parents hate their children
Some parents have too many
Some parents haven't had enough
Some try but can't have any

For what we have is always wrong
Too light, too dark, too short, too long
The cup half empty, glass half full
The day too cold, the sky too dull

Then what we have we wish away
We miss the value of the day
The precious moment gone for ever
Not appreciated, never
Those faults we find we place above
The reasons why it should be love

Extended to our dearest friends
And family, and in the end

My message to you one and all
One day your maker will come to call
Too late then to make amends
For loss of family and friends

And like my mother long since gone
Dear memories, fading, one by one
Of my life I would give one year
For one day with my mother here
To talk, to smile, to smell the hay
And love again, for just one day.

Go on Dad...Knock!

Chapter Eleven: Elizabeth 'Betty' Clark

When I first met Margaret Parr, she told me that she had a story or two about her late husband, Harry Parr (my cousin), and Mother. Both Harry and Mother were characters, and the two of them weren't only relatives; they were good friends.

Back in the 1960s, Harry was at Caryl Gardens, visiting his sister, Flo. Mother was there, too. Harry was unhappy that he couldn't go out for a beer. He was broke. Mother pointed to the fireplace. Next to the pictures and ornaments was a silver coin. It was a 'half-crown' – more than enough for a few hours in the pub way back then. 'Take that,' said Mother.

'Are you sure?' said Harry.

'Of course, go and enjoy yourself,' replied Mother.

Harry thanked her and skipped off to the pub, delighted by his Auntie Betty's generous gesture.

Moments later Flo came into the living room. The milkman was at the door. 'Has anyone seen the half-crown that I left on the mantle-piece for the milkman?' she asked, bewildered that her money seemed to have disappeared.

Mother smiled, shrugged her shoulders. 'Oh, that. I'm afraid I gave it to Harry to lift his spirits so to speak.'

Flo glared at Mother, waiting for more of an explanation than that.

Mother simply said, "Harry needed some cheering up but didn't have any money. I saw the half-crown, gave it to him, and now he's enjoying an afternoon in the pub.' Mother had a heart of gold, but it wasn't her gold that she had been so generous with. Typically, her minor crime was not committed to benefit herself, but that didn't help Flo.

Flo wasn't amused. 'That was my money, not yours, to give. Now what am I going to do about the milkman?' She stomped her foot and marched out of the room without giving Mother a chance to answer.

Mother was a free spirit. She cared that Harry had a good time even if that meant a few rules had to be broken.

Mothers approach to other people's property occasionally went beyond having some fun at the expense of her relatives. Some of the details in our information requested from Social Services made for grim reading. On 29 June 1937 at the age of eighteen, Mother was charged with stealing cash. She was put on probation for one year. In February 1938, she stole a coat and a collection box, breaking the terms of her probation. She was sent to prison for one day.

Later that year she was given probation for twelve months after stealing a blanket and two sheets. In October 1939 she was given three years borstal for 'larceny' (theft) from gas meters. In May 1947, the theft of shoes resulted in two months jail. A March 1948 arrest report reads, 'stole dress from shop' and 'sentence: three months.' In February 1950, her theft of five tablecloths landed her in jail for a further three months, and in November the same year, another case of theft put her back inside for six months. I don't know whether Mother was a very good thief who stole frequently and got caught occasionally, or whether she was such an amateur that she was often apprehended.

But for every one of Mother's crimes, there was a victim, and I would never trivialise nor justify Mother's misdeeds. That said, when I reflect on her actions, I feel more sadness than shame.

It's difficult to reconcile this information with the memory of the woman I knew for the first eight years of my life. Mother gave me everything she had during that time. She was far from materialistic. She had absolutely nothing excluding the bare necessities. Her joys were reading, music and poetry. I can't imagine her having to go through the trauma and embarrassment when being caught stealing, having to appear in court and serving time behind bars.

I now have a better understanding as to why my Christmas presents were the envy of my classmates. If I'm to feel uneasy about the methods used to obtain them, then it's tempered by an even deeper sense of love towards Mother, who was willing to go to these lengths to make me happy.

Her correspondence with Social Services is littered with letters making stern demands for her to make financial contributions to her children's upkeep. It's clear that she wasn't always able to meet those demands. Sometimes she was being asked to contribute more money to the authorities than she was earning. How could she give money to Social Services when she had barely enough money to live a life of impoverishment? The files revealed letters that she had written to Social Services in response to those demands. They provide a window into her mind-set. She took on various jobs to survive *and* satisfy the authorities. She clearly understood the pressure on her to provide. Shortly after she left me, she wrote this letter to Social Services from the Argyle Hotel in Douglas, Isle of Man, where she had found a job:

> *Dear Sir,*
>
> *I am writing to let you know that I have started work, and will be able to do something about Ronald's payment. Now I only started on Tuesday, and my wage is five pounds.*

Will you please let me know just how much I will pay? I am willing to pay £1.5s. Will that be enough? If not will you let me know?

How is Ronald doing? I do hope he is getting along alright. I think of him every day, he is always in my mind. I just can't forget what I did leaving him like that. Well, the damage is done and I can't alter things. I was told he is going on his holidays in August; will it be alright if I send him some spending money? I would like to.

Yours sincerely E Clark

She wrote this letter to Miss Hughes, my social worker, from the Manor House Hotel in Thornton in Craven near Skipton, where she had taken a job:

Dear Miss Hughes,

I am writing this letter to say how much I appreciate your kindness in getting Ronald a new rigout. He must look very smart in it.

You know I can't thank you enough you have all shown kindness that I cannot easily forget, and won't forget ever. He loves living with Mrs Foy and I think she is an ideal person for my boy. She has asked me to make her house mine as well, but no matter how kind a person is I couldn't bring myself to do that so I will just carry on working.

If you ever want extra money for Ronald's keep I will gladly give it. I love my boy and wouldn't like him to be brought up in any other home than where he is now. I must close now,

Yours Sincerely, E Clark'

Through her words, I could see a glimpse of the person I remembered from my childhood, warm and caring. These letters were a re-affirmation that there was a side to Mother that couldn't be seen in the cold, harsh letters and reports in front of me.

Yet, there do not appear to be any letters or financial demands relating to the man who fathered Jean and me: Charles Williams. He is as invisible in the documentation as he was in real life. For all the letters pursuing Mother to contribute to my welfare, there is no sign that any pressure was put on him. At the inquest of my Mother's death, he stated that their relationship lasted for thirty years, albeit on and off.

Over that time span, he stated that she would 'Sometimes leave him.' Mother, sadly wrote in her suicide note that he would, 'Throw her out' when she fell pregnant to him or when she had no money. If this was the case, then it appears that Mother had a 'plan B': the other man in her life, Ah Moy Yong.

Ah Moy was a Chinese seaman who worked for the Blue Funnel Line. He was the father of the twins, Ray and Irene. Social Services' records seem to reveal a good and loving man who cared for the welfare of his children, but who had difficulty maintaining his parental responsibilities because he had to go back to sea, commuting between China and Liverpool.

There appeared to be evidence of a loving relationship between Mother and Ah Moy, yet it seemed that Mother would return to Charles periodically. Whether this was out of a sense of duty, love, or simply that he had a hold over her is impossible to know. It was another aspect of Mother's troubled life that didn't function normally.

When in 1957, Charles Williams wrote the letter to Jean that Social Services retained, offering to meet her, Mother (it appears) was co-habiting with Ah Moy. They were in the process of trying to set up a home and get her children together. Yet during this period, Mother was pregnant and not to Ah Moy but to Charles Williams.

I was the unborn child.

Ah Moy and Mother had been attempting to persuade Social Services to let them take Raymond and Irene back, in the hope that they could set up a home together. They were campaigning to the housing department to get a place. But Social Services intervened, and they were refused a property. The request to reunite them with the twins was rejected. They didn't look kindly at Mother's track record.

If things had been different — if Social Services had been willing to take a chance on Mother and keep her children with her under their support — then maybe this was their opportunity to establish a home and a family. When this didn't happen, the twins stayed in care, moving from one home to another, sometimes together, sometimes apart.

By this time Jean had left Fazakerley Cottage Homes and set up home with Alan, her lifelong partner and husband. Roy, too, had left Fazakerley and gone on to be adopted prior to his career in the Merchant Navy.

But events in 1957 were to take a turn for the worse. Mother and Ah Moy moved into Kent Gardens. They would have been lodging with Joey Moore, in a single room flat sharing a bathroom and a kitchen.

Shortly after the refusal to allow the couple custody of their children, Ah Moy took ill. He was admitted to Liverpool Southern Hospital where he was diagnosed with terminal stomach cancer. Mother visited him while he was hospitalised. On August 27th of that year, I was born. It's difficult to imagine how Mother and Ah Moy must have coped during this period. In October 1957 he discharged himself from hospital and returned home. He died two months later.

§§§

Mother had lost the man who had truly loved her and was trying to give her the support she so lacked. And now she had another child. I wanted to believe that our years together represented a stable period of her tough life, a period of calmer waters. But the first eight years of my life, our life in the 'Tennies,' was to be Mother's last decade on earth. I didn't find answers to the questions surrounding Mother's death. Maybe there wasn't anything to find. In looking for answers to something so tragic it's possible that I looked too hard, trying to find things that weren't really there. But the questions remain. And I couldn't trace Charles Williams. Assuming he has now departed, whatever he knew about his turbulent but long-standing relationship with Mother, he has taken with him.

So, I would hold dear the precious memories of Mother and our brief time together. Of night walks and Beatles songs, of poetry and laughter. And I would forever struggle to hold back a tear whenever I hear 'In the Bleak Midwinter.'

Then one day, it would become my mission to find the siblings that, for most of my life, I knew nothing of, and who hadn't spent time with Mother as I had. And I would pass onto them the stories of Betty Clark, whose troubled journey was so at odds with the gentle, funny, little lady that I knew and adored. And this would be my legacy.

Go on Dad...Knock!

From a life in 'The Tennies,'
In Liverpool one,
Where a poor lone mother,
Tried to bring up her son,

To a lifelong adventure,
A mission to find,
Those family that life
Had left so far behind.

To the joy of a sister,
And to know there are more,
Then meet one more sibling,
And learn there are four,

To a family together,
One beautiful clan,
The happiest prize,
And to think it began,

From a walk up a path,
The clang of a gate,
The sound of the children,
Not wanting to wait,
The anticipation,
Not knowing for sure,
The mystery waiting,
Behind the front door,

Now the size of our family,
No longer a shock,
That began when two kids shouted:
'GO ON DAD...KNOCK!'

Author Biography

Ron Clark was born in Liverpool and lives in Bootle, Merseyside, with his second wife, Ann.

He has two daughters, two step-daughters and a stepson. Ron has spent most of his life working in the automotive industry, having run his own small business for many years. His loves are football, fishing and music when his business allows.

He attends the gym regularly, marching past the various weights and machines in order to put the world to rights with his friends in his beloved sauna.

A few years ago, he teamed up with some old friends to form a group in which he played the bass guitar, and, when the band broke up in August 2015, he decided to use his spare creative time to write this, his one and only, book.